Lessons from Sarajevo

LESSONS FROM SARAJEVO

A War Stories Primer

Jim Hicks

UNIVERSITY OF MASSACHUSETTS PRESS
Amherst and Boston

Copyright © 2013 by University of Massachusetts Press
All rights reserved
Printed in the United States of America

ISBN 978-1-62534-001-6 (paper); 000-9 (hardcover)
Designed by Sally Nichols
Set in Quadraat Open Type
Printed and bound by Thomson-Shore, Inc.

Library of Congress Cataloging-in-Publication Data

Hicks, Jim, 1959–
  Lessons from Sarajevo : a war stories primer / Jim Hicks.
    pages cm.
  Includes bibliographical references and index.
  ISBN 978-1-62534-001-6 (pbk. : alk. paper) — ISBN 978-1-62534-000-9 (hardcover : alk.
paper) 1. War stories, English—History and criticism. 2. War stories, American—History
and criticism. 3. War and literature—Great Britain. 4. War and literature—United States.
5. War in literature. I. Title.
  PR408.W37H53 2013
  820.9′3581—dc23
                        2013002454

British Library Cataloguing-in-Publication Data
A catalogue record for this book is available from the British Library.

for my mother, to my father

Contents

Preface ix

1. Case Study: Of Phantom Nations   1
2. Thesis: The Crime of the Scene   23
3. Victims: The Talking Dead   43
4. Observers: The Real War and the Books   69
5. Aggressors: The Beast Is Back   105
Conclusion: Bringing the Stories Home   125

Notes   167
Works Cited   175
Index   183

Preface

This is not a book about war. It is, in point of fact, a book written by someone who doesn't know a thing about war. When I teach my War Stories class at the University of Massachusetts—as I have now for ten years running—starting with a similar caveat is a matter of clarity, as well as courtesy. I often have a few vets in the room, and usually students with nonprofessional experience of war zones as well. For either group, I'm not certain that I—or the course itself—has anything much to teach them. That has to be their decision, not mine. They no doubt have things to tell us.

Next, I do an informal poll, asking the students a simple question: How many of them have been to war themselves, or have a close friend or family member who has? Inevitably the majority raise their hands, often closer to three-quarters. I teach at a state university, after all. It's essential for this group, I think, to see the other hands raised, and to know that I am not of their tribe.

Having established these two points, I have also triangulated my intended audience, for this book as well as the course. To be frank, it's people like me—those who came to this subject by chance, who didn't know what they were getting into, and who may even decide to stay. The others will make up their own minds—whether any of this sounds familiar, and whether it helps them find their own words. You all, though, the know-nothings, the people like me, you're the ones who absolutely do need to be here. If you don't know why, but you're still reading anyway, well . . . that's a sign you're on the right track.

Most books, I imagine, don't have a date of birth. This one does: January 1, 1997, the day I first arrived in Sarajevo, the capital of Bosnia-Herzegovina, one of seven new states to emerge from the former Yugoslavia. At that time, it was roughly a year after the end of the Bosnian war. And if it weren't for my sister, I might never have set foot there. My wife and I were in Italy, at her family home. My sister Peggy had moved from her job in Zagreb, during the war, to begin work in Sarajevo, where she would live for the next three years. She spent that Christmas with us, and afterward it seemed natural enough to go back with her for a visit. Family solidarity. Since then, I've just kept going. For anyone who's been there in recent years, and even more so, I imagine, for those who were there during the war, I won't need to explain why.

For the rest of you, some explanation is in order. Many, even most, of the war stories discussed below come out of those wars, the war in Bosnia-Herzegovina in particular. Why that war? The dark yet undeniable truth is that other choices aren't lacking. Yet few conflicts rival the siege of Sarajevo for the quantity or the variety of its representations in news, film, photography, and print. On one occasion, while it was still happening, the Bosnian journalist Ozren Kebo found a porno tape titled *Sarajevo* in a Milanese street market. He commented bitterly that "Sarajevo is becoming a brand name, like Benetton, Coca-Cola and Nike." Twenty years on, that brand is less likely to move merchandise in the more obscene corners of our globalized world, but the issue Kebo makes clear remains. So why call this book *Lessons from Sarajevo*?

The short answer is that obscenity and exploitation in war stories will be a key subject, and Bosnians like Kebo have much to teach us about it. This theme is also the heart of Adisa Bašić's short, devastating poem "Trauma Market":

> Aren't you just another victim
> peddling your trauma?
> a Harvard blonde,
> with a brain valued at half a mil',
> asked me.
>
> I didn't know how to reply in English,
> Are you even aware of how right you are?
> Nine deaths from the eardrum —
> Writhing between bullets —

all fit into the word "trauma."

And yes, I couldn't say in English,
I am afraid
that is the only valuable thing I have.

Given her subject, Bašić seems to say, exploitation is indeed an ever-present possibility—and yet her response is not to avoid or censor. Instead she puts the issue squarely on the table.

There is also a strong argument for examining in depth a single war, particularly one where global media were so insistently focused. The whole world was also watching in other times and places (say, during the U.S. war in Vietnam, or the dirty wars of the Southern Cone), yet few moments in history have had—in real time—an equivalent level of media attention together with an engaged community of local filmmakers, musicians, and artists who attempted to shape the international response. The first lesson from Sarajevo is clear: media coverage and artistic engagement will not suffice. This time we knew, and still the longest siege in European history took place.

A few days after September 11, 2001, a reporter on National Public Radio did an interview with Fran Lebowitz. Best known for her ironic commentaries on daily life in the United States, Lebowitz was not, perhaps, the obvious choice for an interview; yet for many she is the quintessential New Yorker, and her response to the horror of the past few days must have seemed relevant for that reason alone. Thinking back, I wonder whether Lebowitz's wit might have been what the NPR reporter was seeking out. Somehow I doubt it: unlike Sarajevo, America was relatively slow in defending itself with humor. As I recall, the parody newspaper The Onion was the first to do so, some weeks later. It reported that the White House was urging Al Qaeda to form a country, so we could more easily attack them. "Osamaland," they suggested, might be its name.

I found one comment by Lebowitz particularly striking, and strangely moving. The reporter inquired what—as a writer, public figure, and noted New Yorker—Lebowitz herself had been doing since the attack. She responded by refusing the basis for his question. "Writers," she replied, "are luxury items." In such moments, many people are essential for the services they alone provide: one imagines a list including police, firemen, surgeons, construction workers, even journalists. Though help and support from everyone, on some level, may also be needed, the skills of the various professions are not equally useful. And as for writers, well, "writers are luxury items."

We could, of course, dispute this point. Few, in fact, would be better placed to argue with Lebowitz than Sarajevans, the residents of a city that resisted three and a half years of barbarism in no small part through their cultural institutions and creative arts. What this remark brought to mind for me, however, immediately and intimately, was a feeling that literature professors may also be mere frosting. In that instant I recalled a sentiment I'd had that first week in January 1997. Walking around the hillside neighborhoods of Sarajevo, I saw people everywhere cleaning up, rebuilding, putting their lives back together. At that moment, a life with books rather than bricks just didn't seem particularly well spent. The moral to this story is simple. For me, a brief comment by a quintessential New Yorker a few days after 9/11 served to transport me to another place on the globe, demonstrating just how close Sarajevo and New York—and any other two spots on the globe—potentially are.

A few years later, this issue came up in a more general, though less dramatic, form, during a conversation with an old friend, an Italian linguist. She'd invited me to a conference, and at some point we began talking about the differences between our respective disciplines. My friend confessed she had always been somewhat puzzled by literary criticism. Not that she didn't enjoy it, she assured me, hearing a knowledgeable lecture about a great book could be vastly entertaining, comparable perhaps to hearing a symphony performed live. And we're talking about a real reader, too—a woman who I also remember once confessing that the elegant, perfectly balanced sentences of Jane Austen had, during a particularly rough patch, almost single-handedly kept her sane. Both sense and sensibility.

And still, she insisted, for literary critics, what was the takeaway? In linguistics, an academic essay is meant to contribute something new, to add to the sum total of what we now know about language. Does literary criticism do anything similar? No matter how impressive the reading (say of Shakespeare by Greenblatt, or Melville by Sedgwick), what are we left with that wasn't there before? Even the analogy with musical performance probably exaggerates—though not everyone does, or even can, read Shakespeare, this ability is certainly more common than, say, conducting, or even mastery of the oboe. On another occasion, during a lunch, I overheard a historian put this critique even more bluntly, in an aside to a sociologist: "We write about things. They write about the representation of things." Ouch.

I don't recall what I said in response to my linguist friend, no doubt because it wasn't memorable. Yet, roughly a decade later, I do feel as if I've begun to formulate an answer. In the meantime, of course, things have happened. For example, in today's world, references to "narratives" and "cultures" sprout like mushrooms: here, a politician's campaign lacks a "coherent narrative"; there, a new CEO fails to understand the "company culture." We may also be learning, at last, about the real consequences of certain imaginary constructions. Hate crimes, for example, are now seen as social—and not random or individual—acts. When Hutu Power Radio broadcast nonstop diatribes referring to Tutsis as cockroaches, the implication was that certain actions should follow. History may be, in some cases, a narrative waiting to happen. Moreover, when a soldier refuses an order, when he says matter-of-factly, "Sorry, I don't shoot prisoners," he too relies on narrative, a story told about oneself by oneself. Narratives can be prosthetic, supporting a decision to resist.

When it comes to war stories, in short, the stakes are high. After all, in a democracy, we are each responsible for policy decisions taken on our behalf. If, despite the sneers of certain historians and sociologists, we treat historical representation, and even history itself, as a text, we then begin to ask certain sorts of questions—such as Who is speaking?, Who is the audience?, and What are the rules for this kind of talk? Knowing what happened, and why, is certainly a worthy goal, yet a practical first step—and the one to be emphasized in this book—is to learn the language through which such history is spoken. Understanding how war stories are told may be necessary in order to arm ourselves against them. In today's world, our screens burgeon daily with scenes from countless conflicts across the globe—commanding our attention, asking for our endorsement, forcing us to choose sides. What each of us needs—preparation for citizenship in this world—is fluency in the diverse forms of representation (journalism, photography, fiction, memoir, comics, cinema) that bring such wars to us. So that's what we'll focus on here.

In the decade or so that I've been studying this topic, I've become increasingly certain that the essential discourse used in most contemporary war stories was forged roughly three centuries ago—and that such language is well past its sell-by date. Again and again, as we will see, such stories can be reduced to a single recurring scene, a basic structure which defines them and by which they in turn attempt to define the conflict they portray. If you've ever read a sentimental novel or watched a melodramatic movie, you know this scene already. A helpless observer watches as an innocent victim is destroyed by a violent beast. It's as simple as that.

Except, of course, that it generally isn't. And yet the power and legacy of this eighteenth-century simplification require that the chapters which follow take it on, step-by-step. After an opening salvo, examining at length a single case study—taken from Walt Whitman's Civil War notebooks—and then a second chapter illustrating the sentimentalism of the standard war story, the following three chapters examine our subject, first from the perspective of the victim, then the observer, and finally the aggressor. Within each chapter, we begin with the most clearly outdated and simplistic examples, then slowly work out what a twenty-first-century version of such tales should be. The closing chapter takes on this last task squarely, offering three extended readings of war stories that are, in some sense, models for the future.

Lessons from Sarajevo is meant, as its subtitle suggests, to be a primer of sorts, an exercise book full of examples which helps readers see grammar behind the language of war stories. Unlike most primers, however, this one teaches a language in order, first, that it be recognized, then better understood, and eventually changed. A tall order, to be sure. Yet my hope remains, and this book has been written, in the belief that we may indeed take lessons from Sarajevo. Only time will tell.

Portions of this preface and chapter 2 appeared as " 'What's It Like There?': Desultory Notes on the Representation of Sarajevo," *Postmodern Culture* 12.2 (January 2002), and "Narrowing the Range of Permissible Lies: Recent Battles in the International Image Tribunal," *Postmodern Culture* 17.3 (May 2007). Parts of chapter 1 appeared as "Of Phantom Nations," *Massachusetts Review* 50.4 (Winter 2009): 479–95.

Lessons from Sarajevo

1

Case Study
Of Phantom Nations

Long, too long America,
Traveling roads all even and peaceful you learn'd from joys
    and prosperity only,
But now, ah now, to learn from crises of anguish, advancing,
    grappling with direst fate and recoiling not,
And now to conceive and show to the world what your children
    en-masse really are,
(For who except myself has yet conceiv'd what your children
    en-masse really are?)

                       Walt Whitman, *Drum-Taps*

A man is not his brain, or any one part of it, but all of his economy, and [. . .]
to lose any part must lessen this sense of his own existence.
             S. Weir Mitchell, "The Case of George Dedlow"

In 1866, after his Civil War service as a surgeon at Turner's Lane Hospital in Philadelphia, the neurologist and novelist S. Weir Mitchell published his first work of fiction in the *Atlantic Monthly*. This short story, "The Case of George Dedlow," is generally credited today as the first description in print of the strange neurological phenomenon commonly known as "phantom limb"—an amputee's sensation that a missing limb is still present. Its protagonist, a triple amputee, passes his time in hospital by interviewing patients like himself:

> I found that the great mass of men who had undergone amputations
> for many months felt the usual consciousness that they still had the
> lost limb. It itched or pained, or was cramped, but never felt hot or

cold. If they had painful sensations referred to it, the conviction of its existence continued unaltered for long periods; but where no pain was felt in it, then by degrees the sense of having that limb faded away entirely. I think we may to some extent explain this.

It should surprise no one when a fictional character, himself a physician as well as a patient, continues to act like a doctor. It is more unusual, perhaps, for a doctor to resort to fiction as a means of furthering science. As it turned out, Weir Mitchell's story was so convincing that the hospital named in the piece received actual donations in the name of his protagonist, George Dedlow. Those who doubt the power of war stories need look no further than Weir Mitchell, the patron saint of science in fiction.

This chapter examines a different, even stranger case, and argues for the power of fiction as reparation rather than research. To do so, we follow the peregrinations of a personal friend of S. Weir Mitchell: one of our greatest poets, Walt Whitman. In a rather neat reversal, our study of this man of letters focuses on his life during the war, when Whitman spent most of his hours working as a volunteer nurse.

In December of 1862, the poet traveled, first to Washington and then to the Union camps near Fredericksburg, following a report in the New York papers that his brother George had been wounded. Although George Washington Whitman had only suffered a minor injury, and would go on to survive more than twenty battles throughout the war, this single episode would change his older brother's life forever. In part, the poet reacted to the industrialized brutality of modern war; Whitman's account of this trip mentions as his first sight "a heap of amputated feet, legs, arms, hands, &c., a full load for a one-horse cart" (712).

What Whitman did at the front, however, responded directly to what he saw there. In the Union camp, the poet spent his time visiting other injured soldiers as well as his brother. After his return to Washington, he continued do so, for years in fact, finding in the role of hospital aide and bedside companion a vocation as compelling as any he ever had, including that of poetry. "I do not see that I do much good to these wounded and dying; but I cannot leave them," he wrote. "Once in a while some youngster holds on to me convulsively, and I do what I can for him; at any rate, stop with him and sit near him for hours, if he wishes it" (713).

Whitman, in describing this calling, compared himself explicitly to the apostle Paul, blinded by divine light on the road to Damascus: "Every man has a religion . . . something which absorbs him, possesses itself of him, makes him over in its image . . . That, whatever it is, seized upon me, made me its servant, slave; induced me to set aside the other ambitions: a trail of glory in the heavens, which I followed, followed, with a full heart" (Erkilla 198, Traubel 581).

It would be difficult to exaggerate the radical nature, and the strangeness, of this conversion. Until this moment, Whitman had hoped for himself what now most scholars believe of him: that he was destined to be America's national poet; he had imagined from the very beginning that his *Leaves of Grass*, by means of his own all-encompassing poetic ego, held the power to bring the country together. From "Song of Myself":

> I am of old and young, of the foolish as much as the wise,
> Regardless of others, ever regardful of others,
> Maternal as well as paternal, a child as well as a man,
> Stuffed with the stuff that is coarse, and stuffed with the stuff that
>   is fine,
> One of the great nation, the nation of many nations—the smallest the
>   same and the largest the same,
> A southerner soon as a northerner, a planter nonchalant and hospitable,
> A Yankee bound my own way . . . . ready for trade . . . . my joints the
> limberest joints on earth and the sternest joints on earth [. . .]
> A farmer, mechanic, or artist . . . . a gentleman, sailor, lover or quaker,
> A prisoner, fancy-man, rowdy, lawyer, physician or priest.
>
> I resist anything better than my own diversity,
> And breathe the air and leave plenty after me,
> And am not stuck up, and am in my place.

Such, then, were the "other ambitions" that our apostle of poetry was induced to "set aside," all the result of a chance trip to the front. But what *would* be the proper role for a national poet in a time of civil war, a time where the nation itself lay in pieces, like discarded limbs heaped outside a battlefield clinic?

Whitman found his answer in Washington's military hospitals. Summing up his work with the wounded, he portrayed his service as a performance in deeds of what his poetry had strived for in verse. "In my ministerings," he states, "I comprehended all, whoever came in my way, northern or southern, and slighted none. It arous'd and brought out and decided undream'd-of depths of emotion. It has given me my most fervent views of the true *ensemble* and extent of the States" (776). In an introductory inscription, his postwar editions of *Leaves of Grass* would claim that "my book and the war are one," and the stated equivalence was functional. (The view otherwise makes little sense, given that most of the poetry was written before the rebellion began.) For Whitman, the nation itself was gathered in both book and war. The poet's allegiance, moreover, was to one nation, so much so that he rarely even used the term "civil war." What he insistently called "The War of Secession," Whitman believed, offered final proof of what his poems had intuited: "a primal hard-pan of national Union will, determin'd and in the majority" (707).

Of the many hospitals he visited, the Patent Office is unique in the attention paid to it by Whitman's writing—and yet the picture he paints is at least as difficult to fathom as his own sense of mission. Washington D.C.'s third-oldest public building (built after only the White House and the Capitol) today houses the National Portrait Gallery and the Smithsonian American Art Museum. And few sites boast a more varied or eventful history. Originally, in Pierre L'Enfant's plan for the capital, its location was designated for either a nondenominational "church of the Republic" or a pantheon for the country's heroes. During its early years, the edifice contained a national collection of historical and cultural treasures as well as the Department of the Interior. Yet its principal function was to serve as the federal Patent Office; it was by that name that the building was known. The celebration for Lincoln's second inauguration was held there as well; the presidential couple is said to have arrived at ten thirty and left around half past one, though the dancing went on till four. And from 1861 to 1863, L'Enfant's plan to create a church or pantheon on the site was realized, when the Patent Office served as one of forty or more makeshift military hospitals scattered throughout the capital city.

In his portrait of the building, Whitman first notes how "that noblest

Patent Office, Washington, D.C., by Bierstadt Brothers, albumen silver print, c. 1861; image/sheet: 7.8 x 14.9 cm (3 1/16 x 5 7/8 in.), mount: 8.3 x 17.2 cm (3 1/4 x 6 ¾ in.). National Portrait Gallery, Smithsonian Institution, NPG.POB114.

of Washington buildings" had become "crowded close with rows of sick, badly wounded and dying soldiers" (717). "I went there many times," the poet adds. "It was a strange, solemn, and, with all its features of suffering and death, a sort of fascinating sight." The source of his fascination appears in a fuller transcription of the passage:

> Two of the immense apartments are fill'd with high and ponderous glass cases, crowded with models in miniature of every kind of utensil, machine or invention, it ever enter'd into the mind of man to conceive; and with curiosities and foreign presents. Between these cases are lateral openings, perhaps eight feet wide and quite deep, and in these were placed the sick, besides a long double row of them up and down through the middle of the hall. Many of them were very bad cases, wounds and amputations. Then there was a gallery running above the hall in which there were beds also. It was, indeed, a curious scene, especially at night when lit up. The glass cases, the beds, the forms lying there, the gallery above, and the marble pavement under foot—the suffering, and the fortitude to bear it in various degrees—occasionally, from some, the groan that could not be repress'd—sometimes a poor fellow dying, with emaciated face and glassy eye,

the nurse by his side, the doctor also there, but no friend, no relative—
such were the sights but lately in the Patent-office. (The wounded
have since been removed from there, and it is now vacant again.) (717)

If this description appears strange to you, it should. In 1924, in his first
Surrealist manifesto, André Breton gave a simple formula for creating
images, "bringing together two more or less distant realities" (20). Yet it
is the juxtaposition of injured soldiers and mechanical curiosities, yoked
by violence together, which compels Whitman's attention. Note, for
example, how a single word, "cases," is used to refer both to display cabi-
nets and patients. In one instance, a single phrase ("the forms lying
there") is so abstract that it could almost refer to either—the contents of
the showcases as well as the beds. That his fascination increases with
lamplight suggests an eerie, phantomlike quality, as if the poet is haunted
by his memory of the scene.

It is discomforting that Whitman makes little reference to the humanity of the spectacle before him—"the forms"—until the final phrases of
his penultimate sentence. Even there the language maintains its abstract,
ironic tone. "Such were the sights," he tells us. And why does the poet
insist, just as a groan from the injured or dying echoes across the hall, that
only medical staff, and no friend or relative, stays with the wounded? After
all, isn't that the reason why he himself is there?

Though this may seem, and no doubt is, an exceptional passage from an
exceptional poet, the issues raised by Whitman's description are unavoid-
able, given the subject matter of this book. Is it possible to speak of war in
an adequate fashion? What tone should one take? And what sort of reaction
would be proper, faced with such horrors? Confronting these questions
head-on seems to me the logical way to begin. In her magisterial work on
war imagery, *Regarding the Pain of Others*, Susan Sontag does precisely that:

there is shame as well as shock in looking at the close-up of a real
horror. Perhaps the only people with the right to look at images of
suffering of this extreme order are those who could do something to
alleviate it—say, the surgeons at the military hospital where the
photo was taken—or those who could learn from it. The rest of us
are voyeurs, whether or not we mean to be.

> In each instance, the gruesome invites us to be either spectators
> or cowards, unable to look. (42)

The choices described here are not good. When the spectacle is war, a voyeur objectifies, denying the human nature of suffering, and a coward allows it free rein.

The real issue—and the central question which this book poses—concerns what we can learn from thinking about war stories. As Sontag suggests, if we ourselves are not in a position to alleviate suffering (though how could we ever be certain of our position?), then what's the use? And why, really, are we interested? What is the source of our fascination? A much-cited passage from Michael Herr's *Dispatches* is blunt about its suspicions: "You know how it is, you want to look and you don't want to look. I can remember the strange feelings I had when I was a kid looking at war photographs in *Life* [. . .] Even when the picture was sharp and cleanly defined, something wasn't clear at all [. . .] I didn't have a language for it then, but I remember the shame I felt, like looking at first porn, all the porn in the world" (18). Now, don't get me wrong: Whitman's actions, his service, dedication, sacrifice, and, above all, his compassion for the wounded are undeniable, they speak to us today from every page of his text. Yet, at times, it is also difficult to read him without feeling that his motives are somewhat, well, complex. We'll return to Whitman, and to the Patent Office hospital as well, but we ought first to take a closer look at the nature of compassion.

From the eighteenth century on, in some circles at least, a lively debate has raged about the use and abuse of compassion in the political arena.[1] (Think how the phrase "bleeding-heart liberals" is used and you'll find yourself on the tip of the iceberg.) One of the hardliners in this discussion was the social philosopher Hannah Arendt. In two influential works, *On Revolution* and *The Human Condition*, Arendt dissected the sympathetic response, dissociating compassion from pity (which she found particularly destructive), dismissing both as counterproductive, or worse, for social and political life. When compassion is brought into the public realm, where political discussion takes place, Arendt believed it to be subject to a particularly virulent form of corruption. Her poster child for this sort of politics was Maximilien Robespierre, a leading figure during the guillotine-wielding days of the Reign of Terror.

Robespierre's self-vaunted *"pitié"* for *"le peuple"* was, according to Arendt, "something ugly, false, and dangerous," the very opposite of compassion. As Elizabeth Spelman notes, "Insofar as pity can so easily come to be enjoyed for its own sake, the pitier needs and seeks out others in misfortune. The suffering of others is [. . .] kept dangling at a delicious and cruel distance" (62, 65). What is vaguely troubling in Whitman, then, and sensed as pornographic in Herr, surfaced in Robespierre as a sadistic abuse of power, with compassion a flimsy, transparent excuse for his political self-aggrandizement. According to Arendt, the only solution was radical: to rule compassion out of court entirely; "the only way to avoid such risks is to keep emotional life separate from political life" (Spelman 68). Arendt didn't elaborate, by the way, on how this was to be accomplished.

In a brilliant riposte, one that at first may seem an "apples and oranges" sort of affair, Spelman uses the autobiography of a nineteenth-century former slave to answer Arendt's critique. Harriet Jacobs, whose 1861 publication was a major force in the abolitionist movement, had rather different ideas about compassion—not surprising, given that her life was in the balance. Jacobs seemed fully aware, moreover, of the dangers she risked in telling her story. There were at least two. The first she shared with any abolitionist work, including the most famous, *Uncle Tom's Cabin*. Legend has it that when Lincoln first met Harriet Beecher Stowe he exclaimed, "So you're the little woman who wrote the book that started this Great War!" As Arendt described it, however, the effect of a sentimentalized tale of suffering may well be perverse pleasure, not political liberation; when African Americans in the sixties turned Stowe's title into a verb, "uncletomming" was the opposite of emancipatory.

For a former slave, however, the second danger must have been even more troubling. In a word, what pity produces is silence. As Elizabeth Spelman points out, Harriet Jacobs's target audience was explicit: Northern white Christian women. If their readerly expectations only allowed for stock characters—"anguished mothers and trembling fugitives"—then Jacobs's actual voice, and the reality of her lived experience, would be moot, if not mute. The alternative is a view of compassion as "capable of being informed by knowledge and hence capable of change, of enlightenment." In other words, the solution is simply "to make sure that those who are suffering participate in the discussion" (Spelman 85, 88). As a way to adjudicate the value of war stories, including Whitman's, this measure is as good as we've got.

In short, despite the very real risks of both voyeurism and cowardice, we do need to study war some more. How else can we learn to hear the voice of suffering? But such a project faces other pressing problems as well. Sontag, you will have noted, speaks of emotions quite distant from either compassion or pity, however conceived: "there is shame as well as shock in looking at the closeup of a real horror," she writes. Her subject, in this line, is the difference between looking at those depictions of suffering which form a major tradition in Western art and, on the other hand, confronting the atrocities which a camera has recorded. The artwork, she argues, presents us with "a complex subject—figures in a landscape— that displays the artist's skill of eye and hand." The artist's imagination, one assumes, plays its part as well. The specific painting Sontag cites in this context is Titian's *Flaying of Marsyas*, a depiction of the punishment chosen by Apollo for the satyr Marsyas, after the latter lost to him in a music contest. Where, other than the mind of the artist, could that blood-thirsty lap dog in the foreground come from?

On the other hand, as Sontag comments, "a photograph of a First World War veteran whose face has been shot away" does seem worlds apart; it is "a camera's record, from very near, of a real person's unspeakably awful mutilation; that and nothing else" (Sontag 41–42). Yet why should such spectacles, whether they are literal or imagined, cause us shame? Without recourse to philosophical or psychological theory, it would be difficult to answer this question. Jonathan Glover, a medical ethicist who has thought deeply about dark times in recent history, cites Kant as the foundation for any understanding of images like these, and, indeed, for the very concept of "crimes against humanity."

Kant, as Glover reminds us, argued that "humanity itself is a dignity; for a man cannot be used merely as a means by any man . . . but must always be used at the same time as an end" (23). Soldiers, of course, have always been used as means to an end; in recent years, the phrase "collateral damage" has been coined in reference to civilians who happen to have their faces shot away, or worse. Perhaps the most pure form of using

Titian, *The Flaying of Marsyas*, oil on canvas, c. 1570–76. (Kroměříž Archdiocesan Museum, Czech Republic). Wikimedia Commons.

people as a means, rather than as people, is found in torture. Kant suggests that such "disgraceful punishments dishonour humanity itself" and that witnesses feel shame at being a member of a species that can have such things done to it (38). Here, however, Glover himself recoils, and suggests, instead, that we must "blush with shame at belonging to a species that can do such things" (39). I wonder . . . though Glover's position is certainly more comfortable, the social dynamic in either case seems nearly the same. Shame is the emotion we feel out of fear that others will catch us in, or identify us with, a shameful position. As Ivan Illich once suggested, it may be a form of social hygiene, cleansing us from the stench of the other.

At this point, we appear to have strayed quite a distance from the Patent Office hospital and L'Enfant's national church—yet the abject may not be as distant from the divine as we sometimes pretend. Readers of today's newspapers will have noted, if they've been paying attention, that we have certainly stayed close to our national poet's overriding concern. Whitman, too, asked himself what is to be done during a national crisis, what we all must do in a time of war—when unspeakable horrors are committed in our name. In J. M. Coetzee's recent novel, *Diary of a Very Bad Year*, the protagonist writes a letter to the editor on this very subject, asking questions that citizens of the United States are unlikely to have yet posed on their own. Coetzee's character reminds us that, according to Demosthenes, "the slave fears only pain, [but] what the free man fears most is shame." Today, he concludes, "the issue for individual Americans [is] how, in the face of this shame to which I am subjected, do I behave? How do I save my honour?"

"Suicide," the editorialist notes, "would save one's honour, and perhaps there have already been honour suicides among Americans that one does not hear of." (In point of fact, I can think of two: Gregory Levey, the son of a *Boston Globe* restaurant critic and stepson of the columnist Ellen Goodson, immolated himself in February 1991 on the Amherst town green. He was thirty years old and a graduate of the University of Massachusetts, where I teach. Malachi Ritscher, a Chicago jazz musician, burned himself to death in protest against the current Iraq war on November 2, 2002. The case of Norman Morrison, a Quaker whose self-immolation took place on November 2, 1965, on the Pentagon lawn beneath Robert McNamara's office, is more widely remembered.) "In the present climate of whipped-up fear, and in the absence of any groundswell of popular revulsion against torture," Coetzee's protagonist concludes, "political actions by individual citizens seem unlikely to have any practical effect. Yet perhaps, pursued doggedly and in a spirit of outrage, such actions may at least allow people to hold their heads up." Lest we forget that this author, more than most, can be said to have intimate knowledge of his subject, Coetzee also gives his character lines that are difficult to read as other than autobiography: "The generation of white South Africans to which I belong, and the next generation, and perhaps the generation after that too, will go bowed under the shame of the crimes that were committed in their name." We have been assured, in other words, there will be some long days ahead.

Although moments in Whitman's writings on war—his description of prison camps at Andersonville or the battlefield at Chancellorville, for example—are marked by both shock and shame, most of his work seems diametrically opposed to the sentiments of Sontag or Coetzee. We shouldn't forget, moreover, that Whitman included a certain number of recruiting poems in his poetic response to the war. Even if his experience in the Washington hospitals did eventually lead him to find a very different form and voice, he continued to publish these bugle calls and flag-waving verses—"Beat! Beat! Drums!" is one such title—in every subsequent edition of *Leaves of Grass*. "My book and the war are one," he wrote, and he meant it. "Rise O Days from Your Fathomless Depths," a more retrospective poem from the "Drum-Taps" section, concludes as follows:

> I waited the bursting forth of the pent fire—on the water and air I
>   waited long;
> But now I no longer wait, I am fully satisfied, I am glutted,
> I have witness'd the true lightning, I have witness'd my cities electric,
> I have lived to behold man burst forth and warlike America rise,
> Hence I will seek no more the food of the northern solitary wilds,
> No more the mountains roam or sail the stormy sea.

In these lines and elsewhere, Whitman's most insistent, and consistent, reading of his place in history is to see the war as both natural and necessary, that very "regeneration through violence" which Richard Slotkin argued to be central to U.S. culture. He will never again write the brash, egocentric, all-encompassing nation songs that are his greatest legacy, and both his best-known ("O Captain! My Captain!") and his finest ("When Lilacs Last in the Dooryard Bloom'd") postwar lines will be found in eulogies, yet we must still assess the author on his own terms. Whitman was no antiwar poet.

To begin this assessment, we'll need to return to the Patent Office and examine Whitman's fascination more fully. His description of the building, after all, doesn't tell us much about what sort of place it was. One sentence is all he gives us; he mentions only glass cases full of "models in miniature of every kind of utensil, machine or invention" as well as "curiosities and foreign presents." No word about what possessed the U.S. government, in 1836, to dedicate its resources to such a building. Why a Patent Office, of all things, with only the presidential mansion and the seat of Congress as older architectural siblings? No mention of what could have attracted, in the years before the Civil War, perhaps 100,000 visitors annually to its premises. Whitman likely didn't say more because he assumed his readers had been there—or were planning to go. A contemporary guidebook to the "Sights and Secrets" of the national capital notes that "the Patent Office is properly a bureau of the Department of the Interior, but it is in all its proportions and features so vast and imposing that we have decided to devote a separate chapter to it" (Ellis 339; see also Dobyns).

From its opening in 1840 until a fire destroyed the north and west wings of the building in 1877, the present home of the National Portrait Gallery was the industrial-age equivalent of a Renaissance *Wunderkammer*, a room of wonders. Like those earlier collections owned by European monarchs and other notables, the contents of the Patent Office combined a odd array of relics, curiosities, treasures, and scientific specimens; unlike the sixteenth- and seventeenth-century exemplars, however, the National Gallery was democratic rather than imperial; the Patent Office administration required contributions of models from all those desiring to patent their ingenuity. As a letter from the first patent commissioner to the Senate chair of the Committee on Patents makes clear, the essential purpose of all such collections had remained unchanged over the centuries: they meant to display, in spectacular fashion, the worth, taste and clout of their proprietors. The "National Gallery," as Commissioner Ellsworth explains it, was designed as "a perpetual exhibition of the progress and improvement of the arts in the United States." "Here the most beautiful specimens of the genius and industry of the nation will be found," he added, "what American can visit the Gallery, and not be still prouder of his country[?]"[2]

The guidebook offers a description of the mechanical arts holdings in this collection:

> Here is every thing the mind can think of. Models of improved arms, clocks, telegraphs, burglar and fire alarms, musical instruments, light-houses, street cars, lamps, stoves, ranges, furnaces, peat and fuel machines, brick and tile machines, sewing machines, power looms, paper-making machinery, knitting machines, machines for making cloth, hats, spool-cotton, for working up hemp, harbor cleaners, patent hooks-and-eyes, buttons, umbrella and cane handles, fluting machines, trusses, medical instruments of gutta percha, corsets, ambulances and other military establishments; arrangements for excluding the dust and smoke from railroad cars, railroad and steamboat machinery, agricultural and domestic machinery of all kinds, and hundreds of other inventions, line both sides of the three immense halls. One might spend a year in examining them, and learn something new every day. For every article one can think of, there are at least half a dozen models, and there are many inventions to be seen of which nine people out of ten have never dreamed before.

Although they receive comparatively few visitors, such "*ars et métiers*" collections still exist today. In Whitman's time, however, collections of historical relics and other curios resided alongside this potlatch of "genius and industry"—items which today seem to have no business there and which have long since been dispersed among the various Smithsonians, or sent off to the National Archives, or simply lost. The original Declaration of Independence was once there, as were most of our early international treaties, a printing press that Benjamin Franklin used in London, and a razor once owned by Captain Cook, not to mention an extensive collection—the "Washington relics"—of personal, household, and military items formerly belonging to the nation's first president.

As it happened, although the Patent Office served as a hospital for over two years, it closed to the wounded only a few weeks after Walt Whitman came to Washington. This short time was more than sufficient to impress its image indelibly on the mind of our national poet. When Whitman gazed across the lantern-lit space of the National Gallery, what he saw objectified there was none other than "the true *ensemble* and extent of the States." For him, the array of soldiers, a display which itself collected specimens from every corner of the nation, fascinated, not because it differed so starkly from the relics, curiosities, and inventions, but because it was their living (or perhaps dying) equivalent. Like the objects under glass, Whitman sees these bodies as "beautiful specimens [. . .] of the nation." The *Wunderkammer*, here as elsewhere, is a spectacle of power.

Having said this, Whitman's obsessive attraction to this scene may sound even more creepy. Is the suffering of the soldiers in the Patent Office hospital, then, mere collateral damage, a necessary step on the way to a deeper comprehension of our heroic nation? Do we really want to yoke, with violence, the unspeakably awful mutilations of these real people together with a pile of relics, whatever you might think they're worth? How is this not an example of men being used as a means, rather than as ends in themselves?

In part the problem may be ours, not Walt's. After all, let's remember the sort of writer we're talking about. No one has ever read Whitman's lines and not been impressed by their physicality; no writer, one would think, would be less likely than he to be oblivious to the pain and suffering before him. His frankness about the body—bodies in pain as well as bodies in love—scandalized his Victorian contemporaries. During these years, poetry would even cost him a cushy job at the Indian Affairs Bureau; his boss, Interior Secretary James Harlan, fired Whitman when he realized that the author of *Leaves of Grass* was in his employ. Yet its verses went well beyond simple sensuality, at least as that term is usually understood.

As Jonah Lehrer has argued, with its denial of mind/body dualism, *Leaves of Grass* actually anticipates the discoveries of contemporary neuroscience; one influential scientist, Antonio Damasio, echoes Whitman in observing that "the mind is embodied . . . not just embrained." Of course, Harriet Jacobs could have told Whitman that; chattel slavery gave her intimate knowledge of the body as the prison of the soul. She didn't have to. After moving briefly to New Orleans in 1848, Whitman saw a slave auction for the first time, and penned into a notebook the very first lines he would include in his great book:

I am the poet of the body
And I am the poet of the soul
I go with the slaves of the earth equally with the masters
And I will stand between the masters and the slaves,
Entering into both so that both shall understand me alike.

Whatever one might think of such mediation, by "going with," "standing between," and "entering into," the poet clearly sides with Jacobs, not with Arendt.

In other words, when Whitman sees, lying before him in the Patent Office hospital, an emblem of "national Union will," he couldn't possibly forget the suffering that has brought this display of humanity before him. Instead, what he does do is give the body a voice. Since the very basis for a *Wunderkammer* is the belief that objects themselves have power, no place could be more appropriate for Whitman's vision. In the Patent Office collection, the relics, specimens, and models, much like the broken bodies of soldiers, have been stripped of their former purpose, taken from their original context. As a result, they now serve to exemplify a greater purpose and context. In dying, a body becomes object; displayed as a fetish, the object comes alive.

No author more than Whitman has so frequently slipped from characterization of the body to the body politic and back again. One of the most telling instances occurs when the poet offers an isolated word as the single best description of "the war itself"—"convulsiveness." Echoing Alice in her confrontation with Humpty Dumpty, we may think that a war is an awful lot for one word to mean, even if "convulsiveness" is not a word most of us use on a regular basis. It's not an old word, either: the *Oxford English Dictionary* lists its earliest usage as 1879, a few years after Whitman used it in his *Memoranda during the War*. A noun made from an adjective based on a noun derived from a verb—a certain distance seems built into Whitman's word for the war. It offers, not a description, but a diagnosis.

"Convulsion," unlike "convulsiveness," is not a new word at all; its medical sense, "involuntary contractions or spasms of the muscles," was used by Pliny and his contemporaries. Another common usage, with a somewhat less lengthy history, describes our environment rather than our bodies—earthquakes, volcanoes, and storms at sea are frequent examples. However, the convulsions most immediately relevant to Whitman were found in the middle ground between our surroundings and ourselves, in the body politic. Describing "a social or political agitation" as convulsive occupies a chronological middle ground as well; semantic usage began with the body, extended through the body politic, and, finally, was located in Nature itself. For each of the three usages, the Latin root appears equally descriptive: convulsion is derived from *convellere*, "to pull violently hither and thither, to wrest, wrench, shatter, etc."[3]

As an emblem for war, a word that refers either to our bodies, to our societies, or to the earth does seem appropriate, and packed into this lexical choice there is even the germ of a story. The term "convulsion" evokes a phenomenon whose cause is unforeseen and often unknown; it designates a moment where something, or somewhere, suddenly appears possessed, violently possessed ("wrested, wrenched or shattered") by an unseen, alien force. Convulsiveness is thus both sudden and transitory (in this alone does convulsion differ from agony). In sum, a convulsion is a crisis, bordered in time and separated by definition from what we see as normal. Finally, as early use of the word in medical treatises suggests, the phenomenon of convulsion is characteristically observed from outside, although little is typically done, or can be done, by the observer (other than noting observations).

It is his role as "Wound-Dresser" (the title of a poem from *Drum-Taps*) that says most about Whitman's own sense of his place in our convulsive history. As I read it, the poem also speaks directly to the issue of why we need war stories. Whitman was no doubt called upon to do many difficult things during his hospital visits; wound-dressing—or even handing a surgeon the saw—may conceivably have been among them. For the most part, however, the voice that emerges in these lines simply registers what he sees.

The catalogue of mutilation that "The Wound-Dresser" records is truly unspeakable: "the crush'd head," "the stump of the arm," "a wound in the side," "the fractur'd thigh, the knee," "the amputated hand," "the perforated shoulder," the "gnawing and putrid gangrene." Such a list clearly fits Sontag's description of the artist's approach to war, as distinct from that of a documentarian: it is no doubt "a complex subject—figures in a landscape," an artistic, though gruesome, display of eye and hand. And yet, particularly as I excerpt it here, the poet's list also seems to borrow from the camera. Like Goya in his "Disasters of War" series, Whitman states point-blank: "I saw this," "This as well," "This is how it happened," or "This cannot be looked at."

Both the catalog and the snapshot appear essential in conveying the lesson Whitman has to offer. To my mind, moreover, the poet's efforts have also been duplicated in a rather unexpected quarter—through research in contemporary neuroscience. A little over a decade ago, while experimenting with a brilliantly simple device, the neurologist V. S. Ramachandran stumbled on some astonishing results. In a very real sense, however, this work may have actually been begun on a day long past—in December 1862, when Whitman first witnessed the assembly-line efficiency of Civil War surgery.

In his laboratory, Dr. Ramachandran built a wooden box about twice the size of a breadbasket, its front open like a small proscenium theater, and its top removed. He then divided this box in half, front to back, with a mirror. If you were to place both hands through the open front, one on each side of the mirror, and then look down from the top, keeping your gaze on the mirrored half of the box's interior, you would still see two hands. One of the two, however, would be a reflection—your other hand remaining behind the looking glass, hidden by the division between the box's two sides.

The catch is that Ramachandran's patients didn't have two hands. His mirror box was invented in order to investigate the phenomenon usually called "phantom limb," the sensation by an amputee that their missing limb is still present. As noted above, this phenomenon was first described clinically by Walt Whitman's friend S. Weir Mitchell. Jonah Lehrer argues that Weir Mitchell's analysis of these "sensory ghosts" may have even been a direct result of correspondence with the poet, and that it must certainly be seen as Whitmanian. "After all," Lehrer notes, "sensory ghosts were living proof of Whitman's poetry: our matter was entangled with our spirit. When you cut the flesh, you also cut the soul" (10).

Back to the box. Ramachandran asked his patients to put their intact

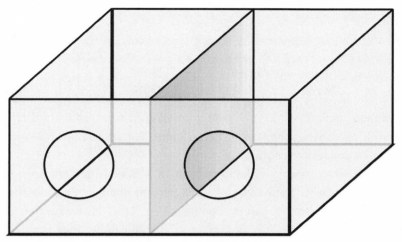

A schematic drawing of Dr. Ramachandran's mirror box. Wikimedia Commons.

hand into its mirror side and to place their phantom limb—as if there really was such a limb—in an analogous position in the other. He then had them look down on the box and watch the two hands—one real, one reflected—while attempting to move their phantom together with the actual limb. In nearly every case, the results were both immediate and breathtaking. One patient, who had reported his phantom as having been paralyzed for twenty years, suddenly experienced an amputated hand which opened and closed, moving together with his real hand. Taken out of the box, the phantom was once again frozen. In this case, Ramachandran decided to let the patient take the mirror device home for a series of daily exercises. The result was something no one could have predicted. One day, a few weeks later, the patient called up to report that his phantom limb had disappeared entirely.[4] "This may be the first known case of a successful 'amputation' of a phantom limb," the good doctor concludes.

So where are we going with all of this? Simple. Knowing the story of Dr. Ramachandran's patients, you should now find the following passage from Whitman's "The Wound-Dresser" even more moving, and more relevant:

> From the stump of the arm, the amputated hand,
> I undo the clotted lint, remove the slough, wash off the matter and blood,

> Back on his pillow the soldier bends with curv'd neck and side-falling head,
> His eyes are closed, his face is pale, he dares not look on the bloody stump,
> And has not yet look'd on it.

Whitman, as a poet and as a person, found his wartime calling by forcing himself to do what the soldier here cannot. His mirror box, however, would be constructed entirely of words.

In his investigation of phantom limb, V. S. Ramachandran notes its startling frequency (between 90 and 98 percent of amputees have some form of the syndrome); he also comments on the various ways that circumstances influence its etiology. Amputations done after traumatic injury, he notes, may be more likely to result in phantom limb than those where the patient (one, say, with a tumor) is prepared for surgery and understands its necessity in advance. Proprioception—the body's sense of its own position, relative to itself—clearly has something to do with phantom limb; knowledge of the amputation is a memo the phantom doesn't get.[5]

Our bodies are whole and immortal, the world is solid beneath our feet, our family loves us, as does God—and our nation deserves allegiance. If we are indeed creatures of habit (and how are we not?), what assumptions could be more habit-forming? There's been a good deal of talk about the spate of Iraq War movies and about the dismal box office figures for nearly all of them. Whitman, surely, would have understood the reluctance of the movie-going public, just as he understood the soldier who turned away from his bloody stump . . . "And has not yet look'd on it." But the Wound-Dresser also knew his own role and wielded a power found only in the mirror of language.

In neurological terms, of course, there is likely to be little or nothing in common between the brain-body loops activated by Dr. Ramachandran's mirror box and the experience of reading a war story or poem. On some level, nevertheless, there may yet be an analogy between our most fundamental—in a literal sense—beliefs about our bodies, our selves, our world, and the body politic. Each of these contribute to what we call our identity: essentially a story we tell ourselves about ourselves, identity is invested, grounded, in the sameness and stability of each. So what do we do, what can be done, when one or more of these foundational strata suddenly begins to convulse? What gets disrupted, in such moments, is a feedback loop, that constant check on our own positioning which, in the case of the body, is called proprioception. Whether or not it has a biological basis, we can certainly imagine an extended form of proprioception, one that includes our surroundings, our family, and our community. And, in history, there may be moments where a nation awakes to find itself missing a limb.

In the prologue to his book on the Rwandan genocide, Philip Gourevitch asks his readers to contemplate their own reasons for following him on his journey. He dissuades them from the hope that they have something to learn, at least in an obvious sense, from the slaughter. "When it comes to genocide," he comments, "you already know right from wrong" (19). He then justifies himself: "The best reason I have come up with for looking closely into Rwanda's stories is that ignoring them makes me even more uncomfortable about existence and my place in it." From the Civil War on, accounts of phantom limb stress its bewildering variety of manifestations: some limbs itch, some ache, some feel no discomfort at all, in others—including the most persistent—the pain can be excruciating. To be uneasy about your own place in the world of the living is a proprioceptive form of haunting.

The nation is, as Benedict Anderson famously tagged it, an "imagined community." As such, it differs in an obvious and important sense from that experience which grounds our understanding of body, self, and family. These others we can see, they are constantly around us, in our face; most important, we see ourselves in them. The nation, in contrast, is all phantom and no limb. Shelves full of books have been written on nations and nationalism, yet the basic question remains. What is a nation?—above all, where do we find it? Does it appear in our newspapers, in our flag-waving and anthems, in our supermarkets, in our travels? Is it all done with mirrors? What feedback loops monitor the nation and our place in it?

The more I myself think about it, the more I believe that the *Wunderkammer* of specimens, both human and not, that so fascinated Whitman during his first few weeks in Washington was a rare spectacle indeed. For an eerie moment, the Patent Office hospital seemed to collect, concretize, and make visible the phantom presence of these convulsive United States. One conclusion, thus, would seem to be inescapable. Only by following Whitman, by daring to look at the bloody stump, only by reading in, around, and about war stories, can we rid ourselves of the phantom.

2

Thesis
The Crime of the Scene

Were there time, it would be worthwhile to consider the style (if one can call it that) of these books, which resemble each other in many respects. In their composition as in their language, they proceed always by affirmative accumulation, never, or hardly ever, by argumentation [. . .] They hammer at an idea, supporting it with whatever might seem to fit, without any analysis, without any discussion of objections, without any references. There is neither knowledge to establish, nor thought to overcome. There is only an already acquired, already available truth to declare.

Philippe Lacoue-Labarthe and Jean-Luc Nancy, "The Nazi Myth"

The thinking behind this chapter began, in some sense, in early March 1999, after the refugee crisis in Kosovo had begun and when the NATO bombing campaign was only days away. One evening after classes, I attended a teach-in on the crisis. At that event, attended by about a hundred students and professors, a sociologist, Peter I. Rose, was the first to speak. He began by showing us a collection of news photos which he had accumulated from a variety of conflicts over the past decades. Each photo portrayed a nearly identical image, a mother and her child, invariably in the midst of desolation of one kind or another. Rose explained, with no trace of irony, that within human rights organizations this image is commonly referred to as "The Madonna of the Refugees."

His point was not, as mine will be here, to describe and reflect on those constraints and presuppositions within our collective imagination which cause this image to be generated, time and time again. Then the case was more simple: in March 1999, history seemed to be repeating itself, and Professor Rose wanted us to think about this woman with her child, to imagine ourselves in her place, and to remember her face the next time

Cover of *Time*, April 12, 1999, War in Kosovo.

events in the world brought it to our attention. And indeed, that time was now. As if my colleague had predicted it, the very next cover of *Time* magazine portrayed a Kosovar Albanian woman, wearing a head scarf and breast-feeding her child while carrying it through a crowd of other displaced Kosovars.

The caps-and-boldface question on this cover does seem bold: was *Time* lobbying for military intervention? By 1999, many published accounts of the earlier war in Bosnia had claimed that journalism was instrumental in bringing the conflict to an end. The notion of an activist press is familiar, of course, at least since the U.S. war in Vietnam: coverage has often been said to set the terms of public opinion, politicians in Western democracies are seen as responding to the sentiments of their various publics—the right pictures are worth, as it were, a thousand divisions. I won't speculate here about whether such claims for the power of the press are true; many articles, and a few books as well, have already begun to investigate this issue.[1] I do suspect, however, that any straightforward narrative of journalistic triumph is far too simple. Whatever the case, even before we examine the effects of war coverage, we would do well to analyze the coverage itself.

The place to begin, as far as I'm concerned, is with a quotation from Jean-Jacques Rousseau's *Discourse on Inequality*. In that influential essay, Rousseau imagined an onlooker who witnesses, and is unable to aid, a mother and child being attacked by a savage beast:

> the tragic image of an imprisoned man who sees, through his window, a wild beast tearing a child from its mother's arms, breaking its frail limbs with murderous teeth, and clawing its quivering entrails. What horrible agitation seizes him as he watches the scene which does not concern him personally! What anguish he suffers from being powerless to help the fainting mother and the dying child! (68)[2]

For the French philosophe, the spectacle he depicted naturally, and necessarily, displays the expression of sympathy—a sentiment he believed so widespread that it isn't even species-specific. From his comments, however, readers today may suspect that Rousseau found tragedy as much in the "anguish" and "agitation" it produces as in the fate it ascribes to the mother and child.

So it seems that the Madonna of the Refugees might well have sold magazines in the eighteenth century, just as she did at the end of the twentieth. At least one literary critic has argued that scenes like this one are found throughout the literature of sensibility, in the novels of Rousseau, Samuel Richardson, Laurence Sterne, as well as legions of lesser-known authors.

Time and time again the subject positions from this scene are reinstated, always in the same form, though not always with the same effect.

Most fundamental is the position that Carol McGuirk calls "the pathetic object," a fancy phrase for victim; she also notes, however, that the viewer's own role sometimes takes center stage: "Sentimental novelists following Sterne [. . .] made the presence of an interpreting sensibility seem more important than the wretchedness described [. . .] The cult of feeling, from [Stern's protagonist] Yorick on, is characterized by a preference in the sentimental spokesman for props that cannot upstage him" (507). Value denied to the experience of the "pathetic object," and value added to the views of the interpreting subject, is indeed the crux of the matter. The third position in staging sentimentalism, in Rousseau's scene at least, is taken up by the beast. Finally, a fourth position—or at least potential position—is made necessary by the prison in which Rousseau's viewer is arbitrarily placed. Although there is none at hand, we may imagine that rescue—and therefore a rescuer—is called for.

Which brings us back to the "interventionist" *Time* cover—in that image, we ourselves assume the position of Rousseau's observer; here there is no question who is the victim, though the beast is left to our imagination. We wonder what violence and aggression, somewhere just outside the frame, could have produced this infinite expanse of refugees. One of the most familiar photos of the war in Bosnia, a shot taken by Ron Haviv during the "ethnic cleansing" of Bijeljina, leaves much less room for speculation: a soldier caught in the act of kicking one of three prostrate figures, all either dying or dead. Sunglasses tucked into his hair, he seems almost graceful; he holds his rifle nonchalantly in one hand, his cigarette in the other. When an exhibition of Haviv's war photos opened in New York in January 2001, this image accompanied the *New York Times* article publicizing the event. The reporter introducing Haviv's show commented simply, "[This photo] tells you everything you need to know."

Three hundred years of rehearsal have prepared us for this statement, so it's not surprising if we agree automatically. In this photo, the subject positions are unmistakable: we know who the victims are, and we know who's a beast, and all we do is watch. (And, in the case of Bijeljina, I should add, the facts did match the photo.) Yet my aim here is to investi-

Ron Haviv / VII, Bijeljina, Bosnia-Herzegovina, March 31, 1992.

gate our reflexive response, to make think us twice—or at least once—about it. In order to do so, we need to return to the eighteenth century, and to the origins of this representational structure.

As it turns out, Rousseau ought to have been a bit more suspicious about the scene he portrayed, given where he found it. In what has to be one of the oddest genealogies in the history of ideas, Rousseau borrowed his "tragic image" from none other than Bernard de Mandeville, the Dutch satirist and author of *The Fable of Bees*. Mandeville, a follower of Thomas Hobbes and a precursor of Adam Smith, believed, like Hobbes, that greed and competition were the foundation for all human behavior. And like Smith, Mandeville criticized his contemporaries' efforts at social engineering, arguing that men left to their own devices, and vices, naturally regulated themselves. Rousseau—crusader against social injustice and fervent believer in the goodness of his fellow man—was the original bleeding-heart liberal, and an inspiration for the French Revolution. How could such a man possibly cite "even Mandeville" as an ally in the quest to universalize compassion?

In its original incarnation, the scene was clearly intended to be ironic—Rousseau, it seems, just didn't get the joke.[3] The French philosophe's blindness in this matter seems almost militant; in Mandeville's text, we are told outright that the Dutch author considers sympathy a "counterfeit Virtue." Mandeville intended, not to reveal the nature of compassion, but rather to expose it. As the scene unfolds, the reader becomes increasingly aware that this horrible, and horribly vivid, description is actually an incrimination of the sentimental observer. With his emotions exposed as vulgar, voyeuristic, even pedophagic, Mandeville's helpless spectator is placed somewhere in moral proximity to the devouring beast. Here then, in all its glory, is the passage as Rousseau found it (in the Mandeville, "our Cries" and "threatning [sic] Gestures" to no avail, we are encouraged to imagine the "ravenous Brute" attacking, destroying, and devouring right before our eyes):

> To see [the Sow] widely open her destructive Jaws, and the poor Lamb beat down with greedy haste; to look on the defenceless Posture of tender Limbs first trampled on, then tore asunder; to see the filthy Snout digging in the yet living Entrails suck up the smoking Blood, and now and then to hear the Crackling of the Bones, and the cruel Animal with savage Pleasure grunt over the horrid Banquet; to hear and see all this, What Tortures would it give the Soul beyond Expression! (255)

It is, no doubt, my unusually high tolerance for grotesque comedy that caused me to imagine Mandeville writing the word "pleasures" in this last phrase, then crossing it out and substituting "tortures." In any case, his closing cements the irony of the passage, returning readers to the theme of fraudulent virtue with which it opened. Such a display, according to the Dutch polemicist, was a clear, distinct and unadulterated example of compassion, one with which, in its appeal to each of the five senses, "even a Highwayman, a House-Breaker or a Murderer" could sympathize (256). That one might well exhibit such sentiments and yet continue one's existence as highwayman, murderer, or indeed pedophage, is precisely Mandeville's point.

Years before he would write his *Wealth of Nations*, Adam Smith also weighed in on this debate, though he would do so in terms markedly more restrained than those of his intellectual predecessor. Smith's *Theory of Moral Sentiments* does find common cause with Mandeville's satire of sentimentality in the distance from which they view their subject. Irony—the distance between what we say and what we mean—is the mortar that binds the Mandevillean opus; in Smith, a similar end is achieved by means of painstaking argument. Distance between observer and pathetic object forms for Smith the a priori basis for sympathy of any kind, an emotion Smith defines in the very first chapter of his very lengthy treatise. For Smith, sympathy is produced within the spectator through a theatrical exercise of imagination:

> As we have no *immediate* experience of what other men feel, we can form no idea of the manner in which they are affected, but by conceiving what we ourselves should feel in the like situation. Though our brother is upon the rack [. . .] It is the impressions of *our own senses only*, not those of his, which our imaginations copy. *By the imagination* we place ourselves in his situation, we conceive ourselves enduring all the same torments, we enter *as it were* into his body, and become *in some measure* the same person with him, and thence form some idea of his sensations, and *even feel something* which, though *weaker in degree*, is *not altogether unlike* them. (3–4, my italics)

Although Smith does suggest some connection or change of position between observer and victim is possible, the shift is produced entirely within the imagination; Smith would continue to envision sympathy in similar fashion throughout his lengthy treatise, according to a careful, sophisticated series of controls.

Adam Smith is likely to impress us as a more temperate, reasonable, and centrist voice than either Rousseau or Mandeville, and in some sense he was. His more immediate interlocutor in this debate, however, was his friend and fellow Scot, the philosopher and historian David Hume. Hume's *Treatise of Human Nature* is also preoccupied with moral sentiments, though to Smith this early work must have seemed dangerously close to the radicalism of Rousseau. For Hume, sympathy has the potential to negate entirely the distance between subject and object, that very distance which grounds the sentimental encounter as portrayed by Mandeville. The literary historian John Mullan makes this point clear: "In the *Treatise*, it is through sympathy that 'we,' the pronoun which Hume characteristically employs, become infused with the passions of others. Hume's scheme of the 'double relation of impressions and ideas,' of their interchangeability, allows for 'us' not merely to 'imagine' another's passion, but for there to take place 'a transition of passion' [. . .] Crucially, Hume asserts that the 'ideas' of the 'passions and sentiments of others' are 'converted into the very impressions they represent' " (29). In eighteenth-century Britain, as Mullan reminds us, unreserved support for this sort of emotional telepathy was a rare bird indeed. The most popular writer on the subject of sensibility, Anthony Ashley-Cooper, the third earl of Shaftesbury, no doubt spoke for the majority. Sympathy, Shaftesbury felt, was a very fine thing indeed when shared within gentlemenly fellowship, but contagious passions in the masses were disruptive and could only be seen as a threat.

So what then are we to make of it when a scene with origins in Mandeville and Rousseau gets jump-cut, time after time, into the midst of contemporary war stories? If nothing else, our brief excursion into the age of bourgeois revolutions teaches us that irony and sentimentality, which we often oppose, may well be two sides of the same coin. Moreover, we also gain a sorting tool: representation that brings the spectator closer to the sufferer, as in Hume or Rousseau, forms the basis for a sentimentalism of the left. Sentimentalism of the right, as in Smith and Mandeville, does just the opposite, emphasizing distance between observer and object. Most important, however, is the tripartite structure of victim, observer, and aggressor: once we recognize the pattern, the very grammar that gives order to this sort of representation, we can begin to track how, in a given case, it has been used.

I began this discussion of war representation by citing a cover from *Time* magazine, that is, an image rather than a story, and there's a reason for that. During the lives of Mandeville and Rousseau, of course, the technology used by photojournalists was still roughly a century away. Even so, there is a photographic quality to these descriptions; in effect, Rousseau's "imprisoned man" offers us a snapshot, and Mandeville circulates a snuff video. The assumption behind both versions, the very idea of observation without participation, where the product of the observation is captured and circulated publicly, seems camera-ready by definition. In the 1970s, Susan Sontag famously noted that "reality has come to seem more and more like what we are shown by cameras" (161); as it turns out, this transformation may already have begun centuries earlier.

And yet, however vivid their images, both writers do stage their performances in words, and they also offer interpretations of that performance.
It is in the latter where they differ most completely. Though Rousseau creates an extremely compact version of the Mandevillean scene, and even
adds a victim (the mother), such changes are minor in comparison to how
he reads its meaning. Rousseau believes in the virtue of compassion, and
says so. Mandeville does not; he thinks those who do are foolish and may
differ little from criminals or perverts. In other words, these two authors
both spin their images, place them in a political context, and urge their
supporters to act on behalf of their opposing causes. Here again, their
texts might well have been written yesterday; they seem little different
from the captions or commentaries that contemporary political campaigns append to images of candidates.

Exploring this distinction—the tension between image and interpretation—is essential to understanding the role photography plays in the
world today. The art historian and novelist John Berger has given one of
the most sober and even-handed descriptions of this relationship: "In the
relation between a photograph and words, the photograph begs for an
interpretation, and the words usually supply it. The photograph, irrefut-
able as evidence but weak in meaning, is given a meaning by the words.
And the words [. . .] are given specific authenticity by the irrefutability of
the photograph. Together the two then become very powerful; an open
question appears to have been fully answered" (92). Berger's words are
measured; they should be read just as carefully. He does not say, you
will note, that when words accompany a photograph, a question gets
answered. He says, instead, that "an *open* question *appears* to have been
fully answered"; the suggestion being, evidently, that the answer is less
than full, and the question remains open.

When, as in the image of the Kosovar Madonna, the words appended to
an image are themselves a question, Berger's caution seems particularly jus-
tified. Where does this image fit on our left-to-right scale of sentimentality?
The question left open above (is *Time* lobbying for military intervention?)
would seem to imply that, as conservative commentators often allege, this
mainstream publication has a left-wing agenda. If intervention is the
answer, wouldn't such an action, by definition, close the distance between

the public view of this on-going horror and the suffering of these victims? I trust readers will remember that U.S.-led NATO forces did in fact intervene in Kosovo during the weeks to come. Doesn't that answer our question?

In a word, no. And the issue is once again distance. Take another look at that cover. "ARE GROUND TROOPS THE ANSWER?" is how the Time editors phrased their headline. We may assume that, at the time, the open question was (as it is now, and as it will continue to be, during any number of crises around the globe) the Tolstoyan question, namely, "what is to be done?" Negotiation, military intervention, or something in between ought all to have still been on the table. In such a moment, to shift the focus to boots on the ground certainly makes a statement, but not necessarily one that collapses distance between the object of pathos and the readers of Time magazine. Faced with this iconic image of suffering, the editor's statement here is best summarized, "Yes, but . . . are ground troops the solution?" And its implied answer is no.

The answer that history gave was also negative. The conflict between the Serbian military and the Kosovar militias, with the latter given air support by NATO, was, for the last group of men with guns, a campaign waged from 30,000 feet and above. The result was unprecedented, so much so that one study (by Michael Ignatieff) of the West's use of force was titled Virtual War. Not a single NATO casualty was incurred. The real cost, less often discussed, for waging war at this distance was anything but virtual; since higher altitudes protect pilots, they also make bombing less accurate, and so the lives of civilians in Serbia and Kosovo were effectively traded for those of NATO troops. The war, for our soldiers and our public, was screened on targeting software and television screens. Others did not have the luxury of distance.

The second image used as an example in this chapter, the photo by Ron Haviv, has been presented here without a caption. As such, the spin it receives—the questions left open and the answers that will be given—are my own. So far I have emphasized its iconic status, offering a comment from the New York Times as evidence: "[This photo] tells you everything you need to know." I have also argued for its sentimental provenance; I want you to see this photo as reshooting a scene co-written by Mandeville and Rousseau. There is tension between these two interpretations. Icons,

Ron Haviv/VII, A Serbian paramilitary unit and their victims in Bijeljina, Bosnia-Herzegovina, on March 31, 1992.

un-like people or places, have no history: they are avatars, embodiments of our beliefs, and magic is granted to them along with immortality.

In the coffee-table edition of his photos, Ron Haviv reveals the history behind his celebrated photo; he also publishes two others in the sequence, before and after shots. The first image shows a woman bending over and touching a prostrate man; the last shows that woman, the man, and another woman, all apparently dead—a soldier from the central photo stands above them, looking over a gate, not at them. Whereas the first shot was taken from a Rousseau-like vantage point, the space between the cab and trailer of a truck where the photographer hid, the next two came from the middle of street, taken as he circled closer to the scene. Not long after, Željko Ražnatović, the leader of the paramilitary "cleansing" Bijeljina of its Muslim population, accosted Haviv and stripped the photographer of his film—one roll was missed.

With this added information, we begin to see a narrative, rather than an icon. The execution of civilians in Bijeljina becomes a process, as well as a reality, one that took time and involved the actions of multiple parties. We see one woman come to the aid of a middle-aged man; we assume that the second must have done the same, and suffered the same brutal end. If we are attentive to such things, we also notice the change in vantage point, and realize that the photographer might well have been executed too. In other words, what the narrative sequence tells us is something we know already, but are encouraged to forget: the sentimental triangle of observer, victim, and aggressor, whether staged in the eighteenth century or just today, is inevitably reductive—even when (as in this case) what it seems to be saying is true. The paramilitary slaughter in Bijeljina *was* beastly, and the division between aggressors and victims *was* close to absolute. Still, with three photos rather than just the one, the picture is changed. Rather than simply gazing at the Bosnian equivalent of Rousseau's beast, we are reminded that victims are not mere victims, and that observation is also participation.

We are also reminded that, in the case of contemporary photo-journalism, the selection of images is where spin begins. In isolation, what does the central photo from this sequence tell us? Insofar as it emphasizes the role of the aggressor, it seems more Mandevillean than Rousseauist; in this regard, it offers a dramatic contrast with the portrait of the Kosovar refugees, which centers on the victims. Unlike Mandeville, of course, there is not a trace of irony in Haviv's shot;[4] it might be more precise to analyze it in the terms inspired by Adam Smith, and to survey what the market made of it. Short of that, given its fame, we may assume that the photo served as a sort of shorthand, a synecdoche for what we were then calling "Bosnia"— the war, not the place (the way we still say "Vietnam"). As an emblem for the war, the image does seem to speak to us. "That's what it's like there . . . that's how those people are, how they behave—it's the Balkans."

Fortunately, there's no need to indulge in speculation about the uses to which this photo was most often put. That sort of effect can be created in prose as well. And nowhere was this done with as much success as in the best seller *Balkan Ghosts.* Oddly enough, though, this particular work didn't directly cover the war at all. Perhaps one day Robert Kaplan's travel narrative will be remembered more for its reception than for its content; it is, when all is said and done, a very bad book. And yet its influence makes it difficult to ignore.

Elizabeth Drew of the *Washington Post* was the first to report that *Balkan Ghosts* had been instrumental in Clinton's dramatic shift to a policy of nonintervention in the Bosnian war; her story was subsequently repeated by other major news outlets.[5] During his successful election campaign, President Clinton had consistently criticized the first Bush White House for a policy that, soon after the election, he himself would adopt. If reading Kaplan had something to do with this shift, what could possibly make it so influential? Here again, the eighteenth century can help us to understand the end of the twentieth.

In a foreword to his second edition, the author himself refers to the story first reported by the *Post* and argues, correctly, that a travel book is hardly a firm foundation for governmental policy. Kaplan also points out how little of his work directly deals with the former Yugoslavia, noting that the book was actually written before the conflict began.[6] Moreover, Kaplan, as a matter of public record, was in favor of U.S. intervention, years before our foreign policy finally moved decisively in that direction. His foreword concludes by reminding us that a turbulent history, such as the one he attributes to his subject region, is neither exclusively Balkan nor a sufficient argument for not intervening. Summed up, these comments suggest, but do not answer, a rather straightforward question. If Balkan Ghosts can be said to have an overall message, did Clinton—not to mention Kaplan's conservative funders—misunderstand it?

I, for one, don't believe that our Reader-in-Chief got it wrong. It should be emphasized that, whenever written, Kaplan's book was published during, and likely because of, the Yugoslav wars. Kaplan notes that it "sold well in hardcover and has been a paperback best seller" (x); this success is, I think, inconceivable without the wars with which it has been associated. When a best seller misinforms us about its subject, chances are that it is actually telling us something about ourselves, something we want to be told.

So how to describe Balkan Ghosts? Kaplan's rhetorical style links his book with the discussion of photographic representation above; it also makes this text an appropriate starting point for any discussion of sentimentalism in contemporary war journalism. Where Balkan Ghosts itself begins, however, is a more difficult issue. Opening the book, the reader immediately encounters a thicket of introductory material (a prologue, a double epigraph, two sets of acknowledgments, a preface, a table of contents, a map, and—in the second edition—a foreword), each of which functions as a framing device, a nested series of equivalents to the prison of Rousseau's observer. First in this list of distancing devices is the section that first begins Kaplan's portrait of "the Balkans." Here the reader is offered an image-laded concatenation that follows the first rule of tabloid journalism. It bleeds, so it leads.

Given that Kaplan's "Prologue" distills, in both form and content, the book as a whole, describing it is also the quickest way to get a sense of his key narrative method—pastiche, or quasi-cinematic montage. In a little more than six pages, the focus flips from a description of a medieval Serbian monastery, to an epic poem, to a novel by Joseph Conrad, to a victim from a Stalinist purge, to a contemporary man-on-the-street interview, to a World War II atrocity, to a second monastery, to the description of a crucifix from a third, and, finally, to a disputed border between Greece and Albania (the birthplace of King Pyrrhus as well as the mother of Alexander the Great, we are told). After this montage, we are at last given Kaplan's thesis, as voiced by a native informant. Let me quote snippets from some of these passages, making a pastiche of my own out of Kaplan's:

> I shivered and groped [. . .] The "blind man is not hindered by eyes: he keeps [. . .] steady on the same road, like a drunk man holding onto the fence" [. . .] Apostles and saints intermingled with medieval Serbian kings and archbishops [. . .] elongated bodies and monstrous hands and heads. Many of the saints' eyes had been scratched out [. . .] "Do you know what it is to throw a child in the air and catch it on a knife in front of its mother?" [. . .] The Legionnaires packed the victims into trucks and drove them to the municipal slaughterhouse [. . .] Blood gushing from decapitated and limbless torsos, the Legionnaires thrust each on a hook and stamped it: "fit for human consumption" [. . .] "How much is such a cross worth?" [. . .] "Rafail went blind carving this crucifix!" [. . .] "Blood will flow in Northern Epirus," announced the roadside graffiti [. . .] This was a time-capsule world, a dim stage upon which people raged, spilled blood, experienced visions and ecstasies [. . .] "Here, we are completely submerged under our own histories." (xv–xxi)

Frankly, Kaplan's prologue reminds me of a melodramatic movie preview. That his form of representation achieves its effects through the manipulation of sentiments, rather than through more mundane forms of historiography, should go without saying. *Balkan Ghosts*, as Lacoue-Labarthe and Nancy put it, works by "hammer[ing] at an idea, supporting it with whatever might seem to fit, without any analysis, without any discussion of objections" (304).

Classified in literary terms, this form of writing borrows most closely from sentimentalism's evil twin, the gothic. The literary historian Margaret Doody has described the imagined landscape of sentimental literature as a sort of limited Hobbesian world, its horror focused around a beleaguered and virtuous heroine—a war of all against one. In gothic fiction, such a world—where life is nasty, brutish, and short—becomes itself an all-powerful force, an environment that threatens to engulf all of the characters and the normally safe distance granted to the spectator as well. Why else would we be afraid? The bottom line of gothic frisson is familiar to every fan of horror movies; whenever the protagonist begins to move toward danger, the audience feels inclined to whisper, "Don't go in there, don't!" Hardly a surprise, then, that Kaplan's most famous reader wanted our boys to stay the hell out of Bosnia.

The essence of the Balkans, according to Kaplan, is both iconic and Mandevillean. In an odd sort of ventriloquism, the central thesis of *Balkan Ghosts* is quoted, rather than stated:

> This was a time-capsule world: a dim stage upon which people raged, spilled blood, experienced visions and ecstasies. Yet their expressions remained fixed and distant, like dusty statuary. "Here, we are completely submerged under our own histories," Luben Gotzev, Bulgaria's former Foreign Minister, told me. (xxi)

A little more than two pages later, the prologue goes on to pose a question which, cited in isolation, might seem almost comic—or would seem so, if this sort of fanciful query didn't frequently have lethal consequences. "What does the earth look like in the places where people commit atrocities?" Kaplan asks. Several pages more and the author answers his own question. Here he describes crossing the Austrian border with the former Yugoslavia:

> The heating, even in the first-class compartments of the train, went off. The restaurant car was decoupled. The car that replaced it was only a stand-up zinc counter for beer, plum brandy, and foul cigarettes without filters. As more stops accumulated, men with grimy fingernails crowded the counter to drink and smoke. When not shouting at each other or slugging back alcohol, they worked their way quietly through pornographic magazines. (xxx)

The author of *Balkan Ghosts* turns quickly away from this scene of dirt, disease, and misogyny, looking outside, only to find—dirt, disease, and misogyny:

Snow beat upon the window. Black lignite fumes rose from brick
and scrap-iron chimneys. The earth here had the harsh, exhausted
face of a prostitute, cursing bitterly between coughs. The landscape
of atrocities is easy to recognize [. . .] (xxxi)

Thirty years after the publication of Edward Said's *Orientalism*, a book that
launched a thousand dissertations, one might have hoped it had become
somewhat more difficult to imagine an entire part of the globe, and its
population, in terms so patently imperious. What the "landscape of
atrocities" should look like, with only a smidgeon of historical sense, is
home. On the other hand, right-wing sentimentalism—the legacy of
Hobbes, Mandeville, and their legion of contemporary disciples—that
does seem easy to recognize.

A more complex case can be found in a memoir by Roger Cohen, a *New
York Times* columnist and the former head of its European desk. His meditation on the war in Bosnia, *Hearts Grown Brutal: Sagas of Sarajevo*, is a difficult text to summarize and even harder to evaluate. In Cohen's descriptions of the formerly Yugoslav peoples, a Kaplanesque Balkanism does
seem to surface. Here, for example, is how he refutes the "separate and
unassimilable peoples" doctrine (commonly used, at the time, by both
Serb and Croat nationalists in Bosnia-Herzegovina):

On all sides of the battle lines, I found similar scenes [. . .] Bosnia
was whole enough, a place where life was always pretty cheap, a land
of melancholy stoicism, of sullen passion, of patient longing, of
sheep-breeding men who, whatever their religion, were quick with
the knife.

There was the same note of yearning in the music, the same min-
gling in all things of the gentle and the harsh, a feature of the Bosnian landscape that has passed to its people. There was the same
preference for reflection over the illusions of action, the same pro-
nounced taste for meditation and observation. (161–62)

There are, no doubt, features of the landscape, music, and rural economy
which are common to many parts of Bosnia-Herzegovina. That life is
therefore cheap, passion sullen, and knives quick—or that passivity is
somehow more natural than action—are generalizations which might

have been lifted from books written a century ago by Kipling or H. Rider Haggard. To have published such observations in 1998 speaks, at the minimum, of a bad ear for language.

Yet *Hearts Grown Brutal* is also an essential book, one that contains sources, narratives, and analysis not available elsewhere. Unlike most journalists, for example, Cohen doesn't see the NATO bombing which finally brought an end to the war as a direct response to the second shelling of the Markale market in Sarajevo, or even to the genocidal slaughter of Srebrenica, despite the fact that it did closely follow these events. Even more commendable, to my mind, is his refusal to see that military intervention as a direct response to journalistic coverage of these two events.

Nonetheless, when Cohen portrays the local population, suffering rather than struggle is his typical subject. Ten pages after a portrait of the heroic self-sacrifice of Eric Hardoin, a French soldier who died while serving with the UN forces, the journalist presents another shooting in the very same street. In this scene, however, an international soldier plays a very different role, one the author describes as "postmodern." As befits this characterization, Cohen's attention is directed at the story's form, rather than its content:

> I sit in Sarajevo's Koševo Hospital early in May 1995 with Faruk Šabanović, a pale and gentle-featured youth, watching a video. Its main subject is Faruk himself, or more precisely his last steps, taken outside the Holiday Inn [. . .]
>
> I was fascinated by the video. It seemed to capture the increasingly surreal and sordid nature of the war. A twenty-year-old civilian is shot on a city street and becomes a paraplegic; a television cameraman, positioned at a dangerous Sarajevo crossroads in the hope of seeing somebody killed or mutilated, films the shooting; a soldier sent by the United Nations as a "peacekeeper" to a city officially called a "safe area," watches. The soldier, encased behind his flak jacket and his galloping dismay, is unable to move because he does not know what his "mandate" permits and, in any event, he is paralyzed by fear. The "victim"—the central figure in the "bang-bang footage"—watches the moment when he was crippled from his hospital bed. (377)

This structural summary is followed by a caption of sorts, an interpretation of the scene's significance. Cohen's next sentence asserts that "this strange collage was Bosnia, and Bosnia had become the dismal exemplar of a 'future' or 'postmodern' war" (377–78). If the journalist is correct to say that his "strange collage" is "Bosnia," the imaginary entity he names should not be confused with either the post-Yugoslav state of Bosnia-Herzegovina or the 1992–95 war that took place within its borders. Instead the "Bosnia" of journalists like Cohen should itself be examined, in order to understand what sort of process has allowed which bits to be selected, and also how and why they are pasted together. Once again, a knowledge of eighteenth-century representation gives the reader necessary tools for reading this "postmodern" vision.

One of the most significant developments in the history of sentimental representation was an increasing preoccupation, during the course of the eighteenth century, with the sensibility of the observer, along with decreasing investment in the subject observed. Cohen's summary of the shooting of Faruk Šabanović shows precisely this sort of shift. Despite his reference to the victim as the "central figure" of the video, it is the UN soldier who occupies a far greater part of Cohen's description, and it is this observer's sensibility alone which is seen from the inside. He, we are told, is "encased behind [. . .] galloping dismay" (whatever that is); he is also said to be both uncertain of his mandate and "paralyzed by fear."

Up to this point, my comments have been directed at Cohen's description of form; the content of the footage, however, is also described in detail:

> There Faruk is, walking briskly across the street, his hair ruffled by the wind. The crack of a shot echoes in the valley. He falls. He lies curled in an almost fetal position. A United Nations soldier in a light blue helmet looks on, motionless. A man arrives, screaming abuse at the soldier, who eventually moves his white United Nations armored personnel carrier. This slight movement is enough to cover the civilian from Serb sniper fire as he rushes out to retrieve Faruk, whose lithe body has turned limp. (377)

I should note that, in representing them here, I have cited Cohen's two versions of the video in reverse order to his; I did so to emphasize the most singularly strange aspect of this "collage." The actual hero of the scene—the civilian who screams at the soldier, eventually succeeding in getting him to do something, and who then rushes out himself to help—is cut from one of the two accounts.

Following Freud, we have been taught to read significance in lapses of just this sort. Cohen's elision also expresses a division typical of sentimentalism. This mode of representation relegates to certain groups the role of passive, innocent, and voiceless victim, while keeping the position of actor for itself. As the *New York Times* reporter himself notes, such a distinction was imposed in Bosnia with almost naturalistic fervor; the attempt was to treat everyone indiscriminately, "as victims, as helpless as the survivors of a flash flood" (239).

Cohen's consciousness of such distortions, however, does not translate in *Hearts Grown Brutal* into conscientious avoidance. There's more to Cohen's oddly incomplete summary than just a missing civilian. After all, what makes an interview with Faruk Šabanović worth presenting, while the voice of the Sarajevan who saves him is not? What leads Cohen to speculate about, even share, the viewpoint of the UN soldier "encased behind his flak jacket" while the civilian who forces that soldier to act doesn't even merit mention?

Cohen finishes his portrait with an elaborate description of what he terms Faruk's "epiphany"—that is, stoic resignation. Šabanović comments: "I know this will be long. But the world can't break me like this. If I remain a paraplegic, I will find some way of dealing with it. I will be better, anyhow, better than the Serb who shot me" (379). Of course, resigned acceptance of one's fate as victim is not the only possible response, wheelchair or no wheelchair—not even within the pages of *Hearts Grown Brutal*. Cohen also interviewed Nermin Tulić, a Sarajevan actor who lost both legs in a mortar blast. The reporter mentions Tulić's performance as a crippled Ubu in Massimo Schuster's 1995 production in Sarajevo of *Ubu Enchaîné*; he also suggests parallels between the man and his role, and the key word he uses to describe Tulić's reaction to his fate is "rage." Yet, with one brief exception—"a moment of lucidity" in which the actor suggests that the war was in fact "an experiment by the world to see how much people can suffer" (364)—actual conversations between Cohen and Tulić go unreported.

Enjoy

Sara-jevo

1993

Coca-Cola logo redesigned by "Trio" Sarajevo

"Enjoy Sara-jevo." Coca-Cola logo redesigned by TRIO (Bojan Hadžihalilović, Dada Hadžihalilović, and Lejla Mulabegović) Sarajevo, 1993. Used by permission.

As stands to reason, during the war in Bosnia no one was more conscious of, or more eloquent about, the costs of sentimentalism than the victims themselves—the very people whom such representation tends to silence. Some of the most prolific, and provocative, artists during the siege of Sara-jevo were Bojan Hadžihalilović, Dada Hadžihalilović, and Lejla Mulabe-gović, their work produced under the collective name "TRIO."[7] Much of it was disseminated on postcards, a method of production which saved paper and also managed to communicate beyond the barricades of war-ravaged Sarajevo. In the example illustrated, TRIO chose, as they often did, to revise one of the most familiar icons of contemporary consumer culture.

Like Bernard de Mandeville several centuries earlier, TRIO clearly under-stood that the spectacle of suffering is an easily acquired taste. Whether containing merely a mild stimulant, like the present soft drink, or a more addictive additive, like the narcotic that originally gave Coca-Cola its name, representations of "suffering at a distance" still remain effective and affect-ing. What the TRIO poster suggests, however, for those with an ear to hear it, is that we have a choice to make. We must decide, in the political as well as the culinary world, what sort of culture we intend to consume.

3
Victims
The Talking Dead

Do dreams offer lessons? Do nightmares have themes, do we awaken and analyze them and live our lives and advise others as a result? Can the foot soldier teach anything important about war, merely for having been there? I think not. He can tell war stories.

Tim O'Brien, *If I Die in a Combat Zone*

Let me begin by clearing up several possible misconceptions. A critique of the sentimental tradition in war representation does not mean that there are no innocent victims, or, for that matter, no acts of criminal aggression. Nor is there some Heisenberg-like principle for war stories, dictating that all observation is necessarily participatory, that representation inevitably changes what it observes (though it certainly can). My simple concern is with the use, and the abuse, of a form of representation that has remained relatively fixed for roughly three centuries. My suspicion is that the immobility of this form also freezes our understanding, and that it continues to do so during a period in which the nature of war itself is undergoing a radical transformation. Failed generals are often said to have fought the last war rather than the present one. What then of the rest of us, who seem still to believe that stories from the eighteenth century are applicable today?

It is the business of art to flip forms—to insist on new rules for description, interpretation, and perception; for this reason, its practices at times seem outlandish, objectionable, even insane. Yet artists, like the rest of us, respond to what is usually called "reality," that is, to the world around them, even when they do so in terms unrecognizable for a general public (ruled, as it must be, by some more general consensus). In this chapter I trace how the engagement of artists has begun to crack the ice frozen around the forms by which we perceive, describe, and interpret war. As we have seen, the linchpin of traditional, eighteenth-century sentimentalism, whether in contemporary accounts of war or elsewhere, is the objectification of a pathetic other. Undoing this process, giving the victims voice, is thus where change in this long-standing representational regime begins.

When Tim O'Brien comments in his memoir that the foot soldier has nothing important to teach, that all he can do is tell war stories, we really ought to pay attention. After all, O'Brien was himself a foot soldier in Vietnam, and he has spent most of his life since practicing the storyteller's trade. And yet, he still uses the expression "war stories" in its pejorative sense, a reference to embellished versions of actual events, stories full of nostalgic reminiscing, tales that are more comradery than chronicle. In this sense, they aren't necessarily even about war at all; colleagues from work, teammates from high school, even fishing buddies all tell "war stories."

The first story told in the first chapter of Michael Herr's *Dispatches*—a book that is about war—has a message closely related to O'Brien's. As setup, to give his tale of Vietnam a bit of peremptory backspin, Herr describes this initial dispatch "as one-pointed and resonant as any war story I ever heard" and adds that "it took a year for me to understand it." Then he gives us the story: "Patrol went up a mountain. One man came back, but he died before he could tell us what happened" (6). That's it. The reporter adds, "I waited for the rest, but it seemed not to be that kind of story; when I asked him what had happened, he just looked like he felt sorry for me, fucked if he'd waste time telling stories to anyone as dumb as I was." Note the language: Herr asks "what had happened" just after he's been told that the only man who knows "what happened" died without telling. This war story, in short, is hermetically sealed; its very point is that what the reporter wants to know, what we all want to know, can't be told. Dead men don't talk.

Moreover, like Herr himself, we should have known better. A page earlier, in introducing the teller of this very short story, the reporter already described the particular horrors that this particular soldier managed to

survive: "It was his third tour. In 1965 he'd been the only survivor in a platoon of the Cav wiped out going into the Ia Drang Valley. In '66 he'd come
back with the Special Forces and one morning after an ambush he'd hidden under the bodies of his team while the VC walked all around them
with knives, making sure. They stripped the bodies of their gear, the
berets too, and finally went away, laughing" (5). In other words, you know
that dead guy who came back?—we're listening to him. So we should take
him seriously when he tells us that there's no way of finding out what we
want to know, that anything else is just war stories.

A psychiatrist (not to mention Samuel Beckett) would be familiar with
this sort of bind. All talk about war is idle talk—since what we're really
curious about was left up on that mountain—and dead men tell no tales.
Yet we keep listening, and they keep talking. So what then does O'Brien
really think he's doing, or Herr, for that matter? What good is this stuff?
And, when it does work, how does it work? What makes a war story effective (and what could that possibly mean)?

In 1992, the year that war began in Bosnia, the Canadian artist Jeff Wall
created a gigantic photograph; its name inspired my chapter title. *Dead
Troops Talk* is, in some fashion, the antipode to the sentiments expressed
by O'Brien and Herr. Wall's full title for the photo (*Dead Troops Talk. A vision
after an ambush of a Red Army patrol, near Moqor, Afghanistan, winter 1986*)
locates the image in both history and geography, and also alludes to the
dreamlike nature of the scene it depicts. The concluding pages of Susan
Sontag's *Regarding the Pain of Others*, which use Wall's work as a bookend,
are impossible to surpass, so I'll simply quote them here:

> The antithesis of a document, a Cibachrome transparency seven and
> a half feet high and more than thirteen feet wide and mounted on a
> light box, shows figures posed in a landscape, a blasted hillside, that
> was constructed in the artist's studio [. . .] Thirteen Russian soldiers
> in bulky winter uniforms and high boots are scattered about a
> pocked, blood-splashed slope lined with loose rocks and the litter of
> war: shell casings, crumpled metal, a boot that holds the lower part
> of a leg [. . .] these Russian conscripts, slaughtered in the Soviet
> Union's own late folly of a colonial war, were never buried. A few
> still have their helmets on. The head of one kneeling figure, talking

Jeff Wall, *Dead Troops Talk (A vision after an ambush of a Red Army patrol, near Moqor, Afghanistan, winter 1986)*, transparency in lightbox, 90¼ x 164¼ in., executed in 1992. Christie's Images Ltd. 2012.

> animatedly, foams with his red brain matter. The atmosphere is warm, convivial, fraternal [. . .] Three men are horsing around: one with a huge wound in his belly straddles another, lying prone, who is laughing at a third man, on his knees, who playfully dangles before him a strip of flesh. One soldier, helmeted, legless, has turned to a comrade some distance away, an alert smile on his face. Below him are two who don't seem quite up to the resurrection and lie supine, their bloodied heads hanging down the stony incline. (123–25)

What most fascinates the author of *On Photography* in this work, however, is what she doesn't see. Despite the image's theaterlike setting, there is no acknowledgment of an audience beyond the frame:

> no, no one is looking out of the picture. There's no threat of protest. They are not about to yell at us to bring a halt to that abomination which is war. They haven't come back to life in order to stagger off to denounce the war-makers who sent them to kill and be killed. And they are not represented as terrifying to others [. . .] These dead are supremely uninterested in the living: in those who took their lives; in witnesses—and in us.

The image thus works in two ways. As a coda to Sontag's book-length meditations on the representation of war, a cautionary note is sounded. Wall, according to Sontag's reading of the image, reminds us that the separation between war and representations of war is both absolute and categorical. As Sartre once commented, death has nothing to do with life. All representations are for the viewer; the thing in itself is not.

Yet this photo may seem familiar in another sense. Constructed, as it was, in a studio using actors and makeup artists, the image also resembles a movie set, as if it recorded the moment just after the action was cut. Seen in this light, Wall's resurrection scene merely comments on the difference between playing dead and being dead, between war games and war. Once again, such a distinction seems absolute and any leveling of it absurd, even obscene. These dead are not dead, they're just working stiffs. In order to play their parts, what do they know, or need to know, about war?

And yet there is that title. When Wall named his work *Dead Troops Talk*, he acknowledged that the bind is inescapable. The troops *are* dead, and yet they are *talking*. Even if Sontag is right, and their real message has nothing to do with us, well, that's a message too. (In effect, Wall's image borrows from the rhetorical mode of *apophasis*, mentioning that which it explicitly excludes.) As in O'Brien and Herr, the talking point here is the pointlessness of trying to bridge the abyss between war and idle talk. Yet is there anything more to claims like these than irony, a cleverness born of nihilism?

I believe there is. As I read it, the representation of war, and of the victims of war, does traditionally tend toward the silencing of victims— toward holding them out as objects of pathos rather than as subjects that speak for themselves. In their own distinctive ways, O'Brien, Herr, and Wall each force us to attend to such silencing; each holds up before us the distance between our own experience and that which we pretend to observe. In acknowledging this distance, we are changed by our knowledge of it; in effect, the object, by resisting the sentimental terms we traditionally have used to represent it, challenges our notions about representation itself. Such moments, when what we have once taken as object—a slave, say, or the proletariat—suddenly begins to speak and somehow makes itself heard, may well be what we have traditionally called revolution.[1] When a war story is effective, in some small measure, this must be the effect it has.

In literature classes, we tend to make much of the authority, of the authorial vision, of a select few voices. There have been many reporters, and even more foot soldiers, yet the effects achieved by the writing of a Herr or an O'Brien are rare indeed. We would be wrong, however, to discount entirely the importance of "merely having been there." On this point, the career of the Civil War photographer Mathew Brady is particularly instructive.[2]

When Brady began his work in the photographic trade, his sensible aim was to use this relatively new technology for creating portraits of the rich and famous, much as painting had already done for centuries. His decision in 1856 to open a studio in Washington, D.C., the seat of the federal government, was a logical development of this plan—not, of course, a clairvoyant anticipation of the war photographer's need to be on the front lines. As the historian Mary Panzer has pointed out, the vast majority of photos which Brady's studio would take during the war years were in fact portraits, and, in his assembled archive, the proportion of portraits to battlefield images was no different.

Of course, the scenes associated with Brady today are those in which the dead far outnumber the living. The most celebrated photos are portraits—if they may still be referred to in this way—of the anonymity of death: the dead at Antietam strewn along a fence line, where they fell, or a line of corpses prepared for mass burial. Oliver Wendell Holmes Sr., who went to Antietam to search for his wounded son, found the images from Brady's studio unbearable to look at. He described them as "so nearly like visiting the battlefield [. . .] that all the emotions exerted by the actual sight of the stained and sordid scene strewed with rags and wrecks came back to us and we buried them in the recesses of our cabinet as we would have buried the mutilated remains of the dead they too vividly represented" (Panzer 117).

A reviewer of the 1862 New York exhibition of Brady's photos titled The Dead of Antietam commented that Brady had "done something to bring home to us the terrible reality and earnestness of war. If he has not brought bodies and laid them in our door-yards and along the streets, he has done

Antietam, Md., bodies of Confederate dead gathered for burial. Photographed by Alexander Gardner, September 1862. Library of Congress, Prints & Photographs Division, LC-B8171-0557 DLC.

something very like it" (Panzer 108–9). From the time of the Homeric epic to that of nineteenth-century romanticism, the glorious acts of heroic men were seen as the motor of war, if not of history itself. Mathew Brady, simply for having been there (or by having sent his cameramen), made the anonymous dead for the first time speak louder than the voices of generals.

Still, it would be easy to overestimate the extent or speed of this shift in paradigm. Until 1875, the U.S. government declined to purchase Brady's archive of photographs; the photographer himself died a pauper. Moreover, if Brady truly saw himself as a portrait artist, rather than as the first war photojournalist, this visual pioneer died a latter-day Columbus—still believing himself in the Indies, and failing to recognize the landscape of industrialized slaughter that he had helped to reveal.

One writer who did give voice to the images captured by Brady's studio was Walt Whitman. A passage from his war notebooks created, in effect, the first Tomb of the Unknown Soldier. After describing the bloody fighting at Chancellorsville, Whitman commented:

> Unnamed, unknown, remain, and still remain, the bravest soldiers.
> Our manliest—our boys—our hardy darlings. Indeed no picture
> gives them. Likely their very names are lost. Likely, the typic one of
> them, (standing, no doubt, for hundreds, thousands,) crawls aside
> to some bush-clump, or ferny tuft, on receiving his death-shot—
> there, sheltering a little while, soaking roots, grass and soil with red
> blood—the battle advances, retreats, flits from the scene, sweeps
> by—and there, haply with pain and suffering, (yet less, far less, than
> is supposed,) the last lethargy winds like a serpent round him—the
> eyes glaze in death—none recks—perhaps the burial-squads, in
> truce, a week afterwards, search not the secluded spot—and there,
> at last, the Bravest Soldier crumbles in the soil of mother earth,
> unburied and unknown. (724)

Whitman's imagined scene, with an anonymous soldier in a secret spot, slowly turning to dust, is transformed into a national unity landscape during the poet's final musings on "The Million Dead," just as his account of the war draws to its close.[3] In neither passage, however, does the poet justify his claim that the "typic one"—a type which he creates—actually merited the inscription bestowed upon him, namely, "the Bravest Soldier." Yet Whitman's sense that isolate and anonymous sacrifice, rather than some superhuman feat of glory, is the purest form of heroism would mark the entire twentieth century, and we are still in its thrall.

It would take the better part of that century for war historians to catch up to Whitman. Not until 1975, the year the North Vietnamese marched into Saigon, was Paul Fussell's splendid study of soldiers' stories, *The Great War and Modern Memory*, published. Perhaps the first literary critic to see the common soldier's vision of war as definitive, Fussell created one of a very short list of books (including some of O'Brien's own) that prove Tim O'Brien wrong.

Early in his work, Fussell makes a brief comment marked by the wisdom of experience. "Every war is ironic," he notes, "because every war is worse than expected." Wars, he tells us, inevitably transform hope into catastrophe, and the book's main subject—the history of the First World War—reveals this design on several levels. "If the pattern of things in 1915 had been a number of small optimistic hopes ending in small ironic catastrophes," Fussell elaborates, "the pattern in 1916 was that of one vast optimistic hope leading to one vast ironic catastrophe" (i.e., the Battle of the Somme and its more than 1.5 million casualties), "known among the troops as the Great Fuck-up" (12).[4]

The most famous lines in English from World War I, and one of the most-read war poems since *The Iliad*, seem a point-by-point application of the Fussell method; they can also serve as an extended example of death in action. Wilfred Owen's "Dulce et Decorum Est," from its title through to its closing line, explicitly takes apart the long tradition of celebratory songs of war. In this twenty-eight-line poem, Owen refutes the Horacian claim—that "It is sweet and fitting to die for one's country"—by presenting two scenes, before and after a gas attack. The result is undeniably worse than expected.

> His hanging face, like a devil's sick of sin;
> [. . .] at every jolt, the blood
> [. . .] gargling from the froth-corrupted lungs,
> Obscene as cancer, bitter as the cud
> Of vile, incurable sores on innocent tongues.

In part, the directness and brutality of lines like these are the message of Owen's medium. Some of the most memorable pages of *The Great War and Modern Memory* document how World War I, for a time at least, appeared to render unspeakable the vocabulary of an older generation of war poets. Horses would be "steeds" no more, dead bodies were neither "ashes" nor "dust," and blood was hardly "the red sweet wine of youth" (Fussell 21–24). Owen's poem, originally dedicated to an author of such pro-war doggerel, did its part in closing the book on such verbiage.

On one level, then, "Dulce et Decorum Est" is simply an effective sally in an argument between poets. Certainly Owen's writing can be grist for the English-major mill; its formal complexity, Latin and classical allusions, assume the right sort of reader. What really makes this poem speak, though, is the dead guy: we're meant to hear that blood gargling, to ruminate on that repulsive scab as if it were a cud. For Owen, a poor stumbling fool—dying because he couldn't get his gas mask on in time— is the poem's center. Here is his description of the attack:

> Gas! Gas! Quick, boys!—An ecstasy of fumbling
> Fitting the clumsy helmets just in time;
> But someone still was yelling out and stumbling
> And flound'ring like a man in fire or lime . . .
> Dim, through the misty panes and thick green light,
> As under a green sea, I saw him drowning.

A quick succession of progressives ("fumbling," "Fitting," "yelling," "stumbling") captures the continuous present of panic; the speaker, through the thick green glass of his mask, witnesses a man drown in the chemical sea. The poem's next two lines, however, mark that death as anything but dead:

> In all my dreams, before my helpless sight,
> He plunges at me, guttering, choking, drowning.

One word in particular stands out here. "Guttering," to be precise, is the moment when wax pours down the side of a candle, causing its flame to flare and sputter; yet here the literal reference is swallowed by sound. Guttural cries, like the drowning man himself, reach out and overwhelm the speaker, pulling him under.

Sometimes there may be advantages to majoring in English, however small. For example, scholars of literature will have noted that, in Owen's search for an objective form, the poet fell back on, and doubled, one of the English poetry's most familiar forms, the Shakespearean sonnet. Almost. As it turns out, the first line in the poem to vary that form is the last in a traditional sonnet, the fourteenth.

In that line, where a contemporary of Shakespeare would have expected to hear a couplet, its clever rhyme playing cha-cha with the "thick green light" from the previous line, we get instead a direct, leaden, first-person statement, and (so far) no rhyme with anything at all. "I saw him drowning." The next two lines—double-spaced above and below to separate them from the rest of the poem—repeat the rhymes of the two lines preceding. And their final word, like a broken record, repeats that of the fourteenth, "drowning." The combined effect of these changes is clear: this

double sonnet is hinged with a mirror, in order to reflect a single apparition, the drowning man. Not so surprising, then, that Owen's image won't
leave us alone either.

Less straightforward, however, is the question of who looks into this
mirror; "Dulce et Decorum Est" presents its reader with a complex
sequence of viewpoints. Its opening scene begins in first-person plural,
the speaker trudging and cursing along with the troops. In the second
quatrain, the view becomes impersonal, externalized, the voice of history
itself ("Men marched asleep"; "All went lame; all blind"). In sharp contrast, the center of the poem is grounded in the speaker's own most intimate emotions, vision, and memory (again, "I saw him drowning").
Finally, its last twelve lines impose a hypothetical observer ("If [. . .] you
too could pace [. . .] and watch [. . .] If you could hear"). With the camera
flying around like this, we might well ask what serves to hold this poem
together?

If you've ever read Owen, you won't have to be told the answer—you've
felt it. The place of the victim, of suffering, is the one constant in this
poem and in his work as a whole; it will also serve to unify the texts discussed throughout this chapter. Owen's poetry captures agony, and it
does so to give it voice, to bring it near, not to put it to rest. As this poem's
conclusion makes clear, the observer here is a position, not a person; a
recipient of experience shared by anyone in this place. As such, the horror
on display isn't that of earlier centuries, and it couldn't be less passive or
resigned. To put it bluntly, Owen's poem suggests that the sentimental
structure of the eighteenth century is not only inadequate by the beginning of the twentieth, it is obscene. The goal of "Dulce et Decorum Est" is
active, even Archimedean, in scope: its aim is to "gutter" the entire tradition that buries our war dead in praise.

This, however, is only a beginning. Although Whitman and Owen are
essential starting points, they cannot, in the main, speak for the victims
of war in the twentieth century. During World War I, approximately 90
percent of the war dead were soldiers, and only 10 percent civilians.[5] By
midcentury, at the end of the Second World War, these percentages had
become roughly equivalent. By the end of the century, civilian deaths

often outnumbered those of soldiers, and, in cases such as Rwanda and Cambodia, even reversed the Great War's ratio. Pause, for a moment, to imagine the reality behind such numbers.

Although there is no exact means of counting, it seems likely that the new century will continue, and perhaps even accelerate, the disproportionate slaughter of noncombatants. It is fitting then that, in 1991, the year Yugoslavia brought to a bitter end the celebrations of 1989, Lynne Hanley published the first sustained critique of Paul Fussell's portrait of the soldier's-eye view. Summarizing her objections to his narrow focus on British and American soldiers, Hanley comments that "women, children, noncombatants, and the enemy have an experience of war as much worth telling and remembering as is the story of any soldier" (9). In fact, if numbers mean anything in this regard, it is the latter stories which ought today to dominate our hearts and minds.

That this has not (yet) happened is no simple by-product of the increasing domination of the media by ever fewer global corporations. It is also an effect of the sort of stories we tell, and of the rules for them, first set down during the Age of Sensibility. It will not be enough simply to change the focus of our stories, to cover civilian victims rather than soldiers in trenches. As long as the tales we tell are still dominated by helpless observers, beastly aggressors, and passive victims, we misrepresent the reality of war in our time.

The limits of this representational tradition could not have been exhibited more clearly than during the recent war in Bosnia. From the spring of 1992 until the end of 1995, the plight of noncombatants was the one story the whole world was watching. In part because the victims were white Europeans, in part because the press mostly stayed in Sarajevo, in part because the Bosnian capital endured the longest siege in the modern history of the West, and in part because the Sarajevans themselves were both heroic and innovative in their resistance, the forty-three-month-long story of civilians living under shells and sniper fire can now be used as an argument both for and against the power of the press.

During and after this war, journalists themselves were often the most eloquent critics of their own representational constraints. Chuck Sudetic, a stringer for the *New York Times* during the Bosnian war, lays out the rules of the game with great concision: "There is a method to presenting the reality of war in *Times* style, a restrictive method but a perfectly valid one just the same. It focuses mainly on institutions and political leaders and their duties and decisions, while leaving the common folk to exemplify trends, to serve as types: a fallen soldier, a screaming mother, a dead baby" (xxxii). And the "types" mentioned here, it should by now go without saying, have no voice in the matter.

In the concluding pages of chapter 2, I discussed a memoir of the Bosnian war years by the journalist Roger Cohen as an illustration of how sentimentality in the media tends to silence and objectify its victims. (I should repeat as well that Cohen himself is aware of this danger, although he fails to avoid it.) On rare occasions, this same memoir also contains Sarajevan voices that are far from resigned or passive. Shortly after his account of conversations with the Bosnian actor Nermin Tulić (in which Cohen speaks of the performer's anger but does not quote it directly), the *Times* columnist does offer an example of something he calls rage, transcribing a confrontation he had with an unnamed Sarajevan woman. Since Cohen's readers will never know what the unnamed rescuer of Faruk Šabanović has to tell us, her words will have to do:

> Here things are black and white. They are. There is evil and there is good. The evil is up on the hills. So when you say you are a journalist and so you must be objective and some of what you write may not be good for us but good for those evil people, then I understand you but I still hate you. Yes, I hate you. Everybody is asking us what this place is really like [. . .] They ask us and ask us and ask us. But to understand perhaps you should go to the other side. Then they will give you a gun and you can look out from the building and you will look through the sight and you will see a man. Then you will know what it is to be *a hunter*. And you will pull the trigger and you will see that man fall and you will have the knowledge that you have killed him. That is a fact. A fact. And then perhaps you will not need to know so much about us, you will not need to know from whom we are descended, or why we became Muslims, or whether Muslims are a nation, or whether Bosnia exists, or anything else at all. (365)

Cohen's response to this tirade is woefully inadequate, offering up only self-aggrandizing lines about how he himself shared this woman's feelings. He comments that "by the spring of 1995, like many people in Sarajevo, [he too] was fighting back rage" (365).

If I hear his interviewee correctly, however, her words articulate something other than rage. They express as well, with great clarity, resistance to a certain form of representation. She says, quite simply, that from the perspective of a besieged Sarajevan, any view one gets through a telescopic lens is ultimately the same, that it doesn't matter whether the lens happens to be mounted on a camera or on a gun. If there were more voices like hers in *Hearts Grown Brutal*, voices that reject the position of object and instead turn the tables on ostensibly sympathetic observers, perhaps such voices, and not Faruk Šabanović's video, would have been heard to express "the increasingly surreal and sordid nature of the war."

Yet it is difficult to read the speech Cohen transcribes—difficult in a very literal sense. Following the usual journalistic conventions, Cohen gives no indication of whether this diatribe was transcribed from a tape or from notes, or even whether it was spoken in English. My guess, given the relative simplicity of the vocabulary (as well as the English fluency of so many Sarajevans), is that the speech probably is given in its original language and was likely transcribed from a tape and amended only slightly to correct minor grammatical glitches (such as a dropped article here or there). Why does this matter?

To put it as succinctly as possible, I believe that we hear the voice of this Sarajevan woman only insofar as we attend to the rhythm her words carry, their music. It ought to be hard to miss: her language is scored throughout with drumming repetition ("Here things are [. . .] they are"; "but I still hate you. Yes, I hate you"; "That is a fact. A fact"). Moreover, such repetition also underscores (and undermines) the objections her audience is likely to hold up against her. A second-person narrative embedded in her tirade, reminiscent of that in the Owen poem, works against those same objections: "You will look [. . .] you will see [. . .] And you will pull the trigger [. . .] and you will have the knowledge that you have killed him."

To label such language "rage," one must deny both its force and its logic: rage is anger considered to be excessive and misdirected. And yet, if we bother to think about it at all, we must assume that the questions that prompted this tirade are in fact those which reporters like Cohen invariably "ask [. . .] and ask [. . .] and ask." And we ought to remember that this question—"what this place is really like"—is only possible if one is not from, or in, that place oneself. Anger at being incessantly viewed from this distance, at being a target—or the target country—bombarded by such relentless questioning, can hardly be described as misdirected. Quite the opposite—the anger is directed, it even offers directions . . . and it offers them to the outside observer.

During the Sarajevo siege years, the single most memorable dissection of the difference between views from inside and out was performed by the Bosnian poet and journalist Semezdin Mehmedinović. His work also offers an alternative to the journalistic silencing found in traditional media accounts. In his *Sarajevo Blues*, a collection of war poems and prose, Mehmedinović describes the reception of an exhibition of photographs by Mladen Pikulić. The show documented the destruction of Vukovar in December 1991, several months before the war in Bosnia began. Its site was a seedy café, full of loud music, and of "dazed young bodies, huge stainless steel pitchers of beer and Coca-Cola [. . .] Bloody syringes [lay] on the floor in the toilet" (57). Suddenly "a young guy at one of the tables points to another young guy—the one in the picture crying before the background of Vukovar decimated by shelling—and says, in amazement: 'He's got the same sweater on I got!'" (57). In this instance, unlike the photographers "who come from abroad to collect their fees from dailies, weeklies and art magazines by trading in death," a local photographer "made it possible for a junkie in a bar in Sarajevo to recognize [. . .] that Sarajevo had already started wearing Vukovar's sweater" (57–58).

Mehmedinović calls the engagement shown by the Pikulić exhibition "intellectual morality," a quality not more important than the *partis pris* of surgeons or firefighters, but perhaps more rare, both in wartime and in peace. The author emphasizes that Sarajevan photographers were remarkable because, unlike most intellectuals, they refused to keep silent. His anecdote also suggests that they were especially noteworthy because, despite the stupor and stupidity of their public, they managed to make themselves heard.

Reading this commentary from Mehmedinović, an outside observer may hesitate before its stark contrast between good and evil, its Sarajevan photographers in white hats and foreigners wearing black. (The earlier equation between snipers and war journalists, despite my exposition, must have evoked a similar reaction.) As a corrective to the centuries-long overvaluation of observations from good Samaritans, polemics of this sort are no doubt salutary. Most important, however, in the examples above, is their common refusal of those pigeonholes which sentimentalist representation provides. Cohen's interlocutor equates the position of observer with that of the beast; Mehmedinović, in contrast, depicts a photo with a victim leaping out of its frame, forcing the observer into a relation of equality with him. Such reversals of hierarchy, moments in which one subject position appears contaminated by its traditional opposite, are steps on the road toward a twenty-first-century form of representation.

One of Mehmedinović's most powerful stories of the Bosnian war, it just so happens, is told from the viewpoint of a local photographer and cameraman—and this portrait is actually diametrically opposed to the author's heroic depiction of Mladen Pikulić. In a column in the Bosnian weekly *Dani*, Mehmedinović discusses the story and summarizes it as follows:

> "The Devil and the Rose" speaks from the perspective of evil, its narrator is the devil. He has brought a bag full of fake tattoos to Sarajevo from somewhere in Western Europe and he then sells them in the city. His job is to film cadavers at the morgue for the archives, but on his way he also sells ideas for news stories to foreign reporters. Then he sees on an exam table at the morgue the beautiful body of a dead girl. On her shoulder there is his fake tattoo.

For Mehmedinović, we may assume, what makes the protagonist devilish is his collaboration; like the foreigners he works for, he "collect[s his] fees from dailies, weeklies and art magazines by trading in death." What makes the story worth telling, however, and the central event in the tale itself, is its protagonist's Poe-like encounter with beauty as the face of death. Here is the narrator's description of that moment:

> In the morgue, with my camera on me, I walked up to her, stretched

out on the table. How can I describe it? She was the sort to make you
believe again in the beauty of the human body. Nothing else comes
to mind. When I reached her, I saw that the shell had destroyed half
of her face.

What touches him, however, is not simply beauty, but death:

> I began to shudder when I noticed on her neck a rose tattoo—my
> fake tattoo. She had my mark on her, like an imaginary kiss. My
> presence in her death sent real shivers down my spine. But from
> radiance, not fear. A soft tremor in the lungs, as if my mind had
> transmitted the image of tattooed petals trembling, a metaphysical
> whisper.

In *Regarding the Pain of Others*, Susan Sontag observes that, in the years
since she first began writing, certain ideas about the relationship between
visual culture and contemporary society had reached the level of plati-
tudes. One such idea is "that in a world saturated [. . .] with images, those
which should matter to us have a diminishing effect: we become callous."
She then comments, "Since I find these ideas formulated in my own essays
on photography, the earliest of which was written thirty years ago, I feel
an irresistible temptation to quarrel with them" (104). Mehmedinović's
"devil" would seem to be the limit case for Sontag's quarrel with herself.
As a field for callousness, few could have more fertile soil than an archivist
of the dead in a war zone.

And yet in this story it is contamination between all three positions—
observer, aggressor, and victim—which the story intends to recount. As
cameraman and stringer for the foreign press, Mehmedinović's narrator
has the role of observer as his official employment. The story's title makes
clear, however, that its readers are meant to distance themselves from his
views; its story told by the beast, the father of lies himself—the tale gives
the literary topos of the "unreliable narrator" a metaphysical boost. And
yet this same narrator's presence in the death of a stranger also leaves him
close to a victim, susceptible to a signal from beyond the grave.

No one, it must be added, seems more surprised or resistant to this ultimate encounter than the photographer himself. As the story begins, he
comments that "every director in the world" would be envious of his current

job; he notes that it's a shame, though, that he's lost his belief in art, in "all that metaphysical kitsch." Elaborating, he adds, "I often used to put my hand down on the forehead of the dead, expecting something, some sign that yesterday this body stood upright [. . .] There was nothing." After finding a friend from his adolescent years at the morgue, he reminisces a bit and then comments, "I don't fully understand it, but that doesn't matter to me. I think our senses prevent us from having any experience whatsoever of death." Even after his encounter with the girl, he does sell her story, and he then attends her funeral to take pictures. Rebuffed vehemently by her brother, he comments, "I am no different from this world in which there is no pity. When I meet a man who has real compassion for another, I will feel differently." In the story's final image, the narrator walks away from the girl's grave, rubbing his hands vigorously with snow, a gesture in part ablution but also a test of his ability to feel.

It is also striking how rarely Mehmedinović's tale names the war. There are no mentions of the siege, no guns, and no explosions, and not one word about the enemy. We are not even told that the protagonist's rather odd job must itself be part of what—in an archaic-sounding phrase—is sometimes called the "war effort." Only when the narrator discusses the deaths of the girl and of his former friend is the city of Sarajevo itself mentioned.

In part, because the story was written and published during the siege, its author might have felt that such details, for his besieged insiders, were simply redundant, not worth mentioning. More important, however, is what such silence opens up: Mehmedinović offers the reality of the Bosnian war as a lens on the world. His narrator, devil or not, lives in our world, and tells us so—"this world where there is no pity."

In *Sarajevo Blues*, a poem titled "Corpse" starts by sketching a related image, both brutal and pure in its simplicity:

> We slowed down at the bridge
> to watch some dogs tear a
> corpse apart by the river
> and then we went on

The poem's second stanza is a single line:

> nothing in me has changed

As do similar statements by the narrator in "The Devil and the Rose," this declaration of sentiment works only through apophasis; it protests too much, and opens the door to the very thing it denies. In the poem's third and final stanza, the other shoe drops:

> I heard the crunch of snow under tires
> like teeth biting into an apple
> and felt the wild desire to laugh
> at you
> because you call this place hell
> and you flee from here convinced
> that death outside Sarajevo does not exist

In the twentieth-first-century version of Rousseau's sentimental encounter, witnessing a horrific scene is just one more bite of the apple, and observer, victim, and aggressor are a single triad, with little to separate one from the other. The real fallacy is believing that, in such a world, safe distances are somehow possible.

The sense that life in besieged Sarajevo would mirror our twenty-first-century world was a relatively common perception, at least among the city's artists. Some of the most active belonged to a group that calls itself FAMA. During the siege, this collective engaged in a series of projects designed to archive the events and experience of the war as well as represent it to the world. "Simply having been there," in other words, gives their work its unique perspective and message.

Two FAMA publications, *Sarajevo Survival Map* and *Sarajevo Survival Guide*, explicitly targeted visitors to the besieged city. The map is a brilliant, cartoonish affair, showing the city surrounded by artillery drawn as large as entire neighborhoods, and its streets dotted with stick figures running from place to place. The map's reverse side appends color commentaries for major points of media interest. The *Survival Guide*, written during the first year of the siege, is a parodic, Michelin-style intro to the city, complete with chapters on "Water" and "Heating" as well as one on "Entertainment and Accommodation." The guidebook's prologue is explicit about its motives: "The Guide Book to Sarajevo [. . .] is a chronicle, a guide for survival, a part of a future archive which shows the city of Sarajevo not as a victim, but as a place of experiment where wit can still archive victory over terror [. . .] This book was written at the site where one civilisation was dismantled out of intentional violence, and where another had to be born, the one of 21st Century." Although it is inherently difficult to anticipate what attitude victims may take when they begin to make themselves heard, the *Sarajevo Survival Guide* suggests they won't be timid.

In January 1997, like many first-time visitors to Sarajevo, I was immediately struck by the jujitsu force of Bosnian war humor—so much so, in fact, that for a time I contemplated collecting jokes about the war as an exercise in contemporary folklore. One Bosnian who heard this idea from me commented, "Sure, everyone who comes here wants to do that."[6] When I inquired if one of the FAMA collective might be interested in collaborating on such a volume, I was told that "during the war, the enemy was serious, so we had to be funny. Now they're a joke, so it's time for us to get serious."

To my mind, the definitive record of lived experience in besieged Sarajevo is a film titled *MGM Sarajevo*. Actually, it's three films, each a short documentary originally produced, it can be assumed, for a global audience. In 1994, the directors—all members of a Sarajevo film collective called SaGA (short for "Sarajevo Group of Authors)—decided to intersplice their three films into a single, feature-length movie. "MGM," in this instance, stands for Man, God, and Monster.

On their website, SaGA describes *MGM Sarajevo* as the demonstration of "a new kind of film aesthetics, which could be called Sarajevo super-realism [. . . an] acquired view of life as imposed by war." The first of the three shorts depicts daily life under the siege; the second follows Susan Sontag's staging of *Waiting for Godot* in Sarajevo; the third records the confessions of Borislav Herak, a young Serb prisoner accused of war crimes. On their own, I believe, although each of three films is important, none is exceptional. Together, they are almost unwatchable—which, to my mind, is what makes them the single best record of the historical moment in question.

On one level, this filmic chimera was created from the shards of eighteenth-century representation. Although it performs its part with irony, Mirza Idrizović's *Diary of a Filmmaker*, a chronicle of life in the besieged city, resurrects a standard war report genre, and the position of external observer determines both its content and form. In contrast, Pjer Žalica's *Godot-Sarajevo*—created, as Sontag herself put it "with and for Sarajevans"—gives the response of victims themselves to life under the siege. Finally, Ismet Arnautalić and Ademir Kenović's *Interview with a Monster* is just what it says, a portrait of the world as seen by the aggressor.

What makes *MGM Sarajevo* work, however, is the way in which these three films, each focused on an incommensurate slice of history, each privileging a distinct subject position, bleed into each other. When the SaGA directors decided, sometime during the third year of the siege, to edit together this feature-length composite, years had passed and local hopes for international intervention in the conflict had faded. As captured on tape in a BBC documentary, the siege itself had begun with an order from General Ratko Mladić to shell the Sarajevans to the point of madness. The film that Ismet Arnautalić, Mirza Idrizović, Ademir Kenović, and Pjer Žalica made together contains that madness and transforms it into art.

One representative ten-minute segment, nearly an hour into the film, begins with a middle-aged woman entering an apartment. She greets her small dog, then a cat; later we are introduced to her college-age son and his girlfriend. This scene is intercut with a second domestic scene, a younger couple with a small baby; there we overhear a discussion about basic necessities (food, heat, electricity, etc.). The home-video moment is made complete when the two students, along with the boy's mother, sing a blues song together, off-key, as the boy strums his guitar.

Of course, in your home video, or mine, it isn't likely that the lyric "I wanna die easy when I die" would have the same resonance it did in wartime Sarajevo. A Sarajevan audience, in some measure, must also have been less shocked by the jump cut from these interior scenes to some of the bloodiest footage from the Markale marketplace massacre. Suddenly, amid a flurry of voices, we watch as a woman with half her head shredded from her body is rushed into the back of a van. The camera lingers for a moment on the bloody, no-longer-human mess. As it does, we hear an off-camera voice which is by now familiar, that of Borislav Herak. "Kind of . . . I don't, I don't have dreams," he tells us. "My dreams are, somehow, disconnected."

At this point, however, our interview with the monster itself takes an unexpected turn. We see Herak, and listen as he describes a dream in which "the image of a man who has been killed" comes to him. He wakes up, sweating, he says, only to have this dream followed by another about how he cut a soldier's throat. Again soaked in sweat, he smokes obsessively; it takes him, he says, an hour or two to fall back asleep. At last, however, another dream comes, one that brings to him first his mother and father, and then Sarajevo. "I dream of the city again and again." He explains how he had been in the habit of drawing the city, his house and the buildings around it. "As it once was," he comments.

The segment ends with a photomontage that takes Roy Orbison's "In Dreams" as its soundtrack. We first glimpse scenes from the Godot rehearsals, then various Sarajevan sites, each devastated by war and yet each somehow increasingly postcard-worthy. As the montage comes to an end, Orbison croons, "It's too bad that all these things / Can only happen in my dreams / Only in dreams, in beautiful dreams." To sum up the sequence again: home-video moments, followed by brutal slaughter of civilians, then the troubled dreams of a war criminal, and, last, scenes from rehearsal followed by static images of an assassinated city.

In composing a film that blends together such disparate registers, the SaGA directors structure their work to emphasize the very process which they themselves are engaged in: the imposition of form and meaning on horror and the inexplicable. Hard as it may be to understand, with their edit the filmmakers thus echo the sentiments, and the practice, of the man they themselves call a monster. He draws the city, just as they do. Just as the transition from domestic scenes of tranquility to the daily terror of the siege is accomplished by means of a song, the transition from the troubled sleep of an alleged war criminal to the staging of an absurdist play gets mediated by a nostalgic portrait of the loss of home and innocence. "In dreams, I walk with you," as the man with the shades would have it. "In dreams, I talk with you."

For Freud, form in art is a spoonful of sugar—it helps the medicine go down. Since the truths that art reveals are those that consciousness would prefer to repress, artists distract the censors by means of formal manipulations. Something similar seems to have been going on here. At the time

the film was made, the blues song from this sequence was being performed nightly in the staging of a Euripides play, the one in which Hera-
cles wrestles with Death himself to win Queen Alcestis back for the world
of the living. In their creation of a single film that builds—in this sequence
as in the film as a whole—by means of a slow crescendo of artfulness, the
SaGA directors create a vision where monstrosity, banality, and the sub-
lime may all be, at any moment, present at the drop of a hat.

There is an activism in this sort of filmmaking, though not that of the
three shorts that preceded the feature-length compilation. Whereas its
source materials attempted to represent directly various aspects of life in
the besieged city, MGM Sarajevo works instead against the dominant, sentimental constructions of its story. It cements a new significance onto the
lesson of Sarajevo, one that comprehends, and contains victims, observers, and the sleep of reason as well.

Thus far, my emphasis in this chapter on lived experience, on "simply having been there," has risked implying that such experience is not just effective but also necessary. I don't actually believe this. For example, it isn't the
case that, in representing Sarajevo, non-Sarajevans can't do it. But it does
require a change of thinking, to get our minds right, as it were.

I'll close with an example. Jewlia Eisenberg, the composer, arranger
and lead singer of the vocal trio Charming Hostess, took words from
Semezdin Mehmedinović to use as lyrics on their third CD, titled, like
Mehmedinović's own collection, Sarajevo Blues. The songs written from
Mehmedinović's words often mix genres and styles within individual
compositions; for the sake of simplicity, however, I take two atypically
uniform pieces, from opposite extremes, to comment on briefly.

The first is from a Mehmedinović prose piece titled "Imam Begove
Džamije" (Imam of the Bey's Mosque). Organized as a short list of memories and observations, punctuated by a summary of the religious leader's thoughts on a few specific topics, this selection recounts a visit by
Mehmedinović to the imam's home. From this piece, Eisenberg takes
only the second paragraph, an account of the personal toll which the
siege took in the life of this singular individual. Mehmedinović summarizes with brutal and beautiful simplicity: "Efendi Spahić [. . .] had three

children and a grandchild that were killed by the shells that fell on Daire. Before that, his wife too; as if God had taken her to Him, to protect her. So she wouldn't see" (39). His text adds a brief commentary: "Here's what I think: there are neither major nor minor tragedies. Tragedies exist. Some can be described. There are others for which every heart is too small. Those kind cannot fit in the heart" (39). All of these lines are given in English translation on the CD jacket. Sung in the original language, only the second selection is put to music. A note tells us that the melody is traditional; it is almost a chant, no doubt Turkish or Middle Eastern in origin.

The song begins with a single voice. Time is kept with rhythmic breath sounds and a frame drum. From the four sentences quoted above, three verses are built; the second line sung twice ("Some, perhaps, words can describe"), with its repetitions joined together by means of an interpolated invocation ("Allah, Allah!") used as the final half of each verse. An additional voice is added as the refrain begins, and added harmonies are layered into the following verses as well, giving the whole a slow, spiraling crescendo in volume and emotional tenor. The subject of Mehmedinović's reflections is, of course, that commonplace of eighteenth-century aesthetics: the human ability, or inability, "to convert non-sensory, 'inward' patterns of experience (feeling, emotions, passions) into objects of perception" (De Man 123–24). The final line develops the equivocation carried internally in the refrain: "perhaps" description is possible, and yet, if a tragedy does not fit—and thus cannot stay—in the heart, where then is it to go? Into song? Inshallah.

Jump-cut from the Bey's Mosque to another Eisenberg composition, a piece originally titled "Shelter" (Sklonište). In the excerpt transposed by ChoHo (as they call themselves), this titular theme is touched on twice, first in reference to a group of photographers "doing their job, in deep cover." More importantly, though less overtly, the theme surfaces again in what Mehmedinović refers to as the "almost touching [. . .] comic motion" (74) of "a man [running] with a newspaper on his head on [a] street with a sniper": the singers repeat this line nine times in a row, then use it one final time to end the song. As Mehmedinović comments (in lines not used in the song), "Being in this city means you have no cover, you're in mortal danger every second [. . .] To survive mentally, you need to secure whatever shelter is comforting" (74, translation modified). So why not? If you believe that a newspaper might shield you from something other than raindrops or cameras, at the very moment when photographers, working for the same media, are waiting to score for tomorrow's newspapers, so be it.

What music could possibly express such an image, such a gesture, given its horrifying reality? When I saw them perform in New York City, Charming Hostess introduced their song with an anecdote that revealed a certain hesitation, or at least discretion, about their own response to this question. During an earlier performance in Sarajevo, they had actually decided not to perform the song. Their version of "Shelter" is called "Death Is a Job"—and these are its opening lyrics:

> I'm running across an intersection
> to avoid the bullet of a sniper
> from the hill
> when I walk into some photographers
> Oh well, they're doing their job
> in deep cover

The song continues:

> Well if a bullet hit me
> they got a shot
> worth so much more than my life
> that I'm not even sure who to hate
> the sniper or the monkey with a Nikon

So, I'll stop hesitating myself and just tell you flat out. To stage these lines, the vocal trio relies on the bedrock of all American street-corner singing—classic 1950s doo wop, with a bit of hip-hop percussive backup for good measure. Boom chuck-a, boom chuck, boom chuck-a, boom chuck. You get the idea. By the time they reach the chorus and start singing full bore, snapping back and forth between three-part harmony and more rhythm shtick, you just know that this bouncy little number is going to be in your head for weeks, tempting you to bop around town to its beat, cocooned in your own mental boogie machine.

But wait a minute. Or, as the current Internet idiom would put it,

WTF?!?! Isn't taking the "utter helplessless" of Mehmedinović (his words, not mine), not to mention the entire population of Sarajevo, and giving them a snazzy jazzy soundtrack, one so impossibly upbeat that it can't help but make you laugh, absolutely the most offensive thing you can possibly imagine? Well, yes, it would be, or at least I think it would be, if I didn't instead find it to be one of the most heart-rending tracks I have ever heard in my life. And, yes, it would be, perhaps, if those monkeys weren't our monkeys, if that music wasn't our music, and if we hadn't been the ones dancing in the aisles, and out of the theater, and into the streets throughout all of 1992–95, throughout all of the longest siege in modern military history. What do you expect—Mahler? Samuel Barber? Would you prefer to have a good cry? Evidently you're forgetting what Suljo (n.6) told us: "If you'd had both of your arms cut off, like I did, and your ass was itching like crazy, like mine is, you'd be laughing too."

In the end, of course, it isn't up to us. Charming Hostess, as it turned out, did perform this song in Sarajevo: their audience demanded it—wouldn't let them leave until they did. Semezdin Mehmedinović, when he first heard the music that his work had inspired, had this to say:

> It would not be enough to describe myself as happily astonished [. . .] You ask yourself—how could there be that feeling of recognition, such a degree of understanding, in an American decoding of my Sarajevo story? I have no answer to that.
>
> In the end, I remember an unusual experience of translating: sometime in the 80's, Miljenko Jergović and I were translating, very loosely and honestly amused, one of Tomaž Šalamun's poems. We did it this way: we incorporated some Slovenian words (not ones that Šalamun used) into the Bosnian translation, and called the whole thing a translation from Slovenian into Slovenian. I think that is the method Jewlia used; her *Sarajevo Blues* is a translation from Sarajevan and to [sic] Sarajevan.[7]

And, finally, though it should certainly go without saying: to employ such a method, even to understand why it might be necessary to employ such a method, one first has to listen. And learn something.

4

Observers
The Real War and the Books

The question was never [how] to get away from facts but [how to get] closer to them, not fighting empiricism but, on the contrary, renewing empiricism.
Bruno Latour, "Why Has Critique Run Out of Steam?"

In one of the most quoted phrases from Whitman's Civil War notebooks, our national poet remarks that "the real war will never get into the books." More recently, one of the legends of French documentary cinema made the same point about his own chosen medium, with a bit more specificity. Chris Marker noted that, "As long as there is no olfactory cinema [. . .], there will be no films of war." ("Smellies," I guess you would have to call them, in the way we used to refer to "talkies.") Marker adds that this absence is "prudent, because if there were such films [. . .] there wouldn't be a single spectator left."[1] Granted. When I say "the real war," smellies are certainly not what I have mind. Claims for "realism" in Marker's sense are the product of a category error, and the pronouncement that "there will be no films of war" simply calls attention to it.

In the final decades of the last millennium, in the throes of our post-structuralist, pomo, hip, pop, hip-hop, new-agey middle age, we became old friends with dictates that once amused, startled, or scandalized. From Guy Debord's "society of spectacle" to Jean Baudrillard's "the simulacrum is the truth," clarion calls marched us forth daily into the brave new regime of the sign, semiotexters hung out on every street corner, and pixelated simulacra winked at us from every TV screen. War was no exception (it may have even become the rule). I've already noted, in an earlier chapter, Michael Ignatieff's study of the Kosovo conflict, *Virtual War*. On the other side of the Atlantic, in *Figures de la guerre*, the art historian Hélène

Puiseux begins with Magritte and ends with Bosnia on TV, describing the latter as a form of absurdist dinner theater. A French media center's study of Bosnian war coverage found its own chosen literary precedent in a more distant century, analyzing the Sarajevo siege in terms of the Aristotelian conventions for tragedy. Perhaps reactionary, a bit nutty, or simply sadly confused, in this chapter I speculate about the presence of, not just realism, but reality in certain very disparate accounts of war.

Sontag's *Regarding the Pain of Others* on this issue doesn't mince words. In her opinion, "To speak of reality becoming a spectacle is a breathtaking provincialism. It universalizes the viewing habits of a small, educated population living in the rich part of the world, where news has been converted into entertainment [. . .] There are hundreds of millions of television watchers who are far from inured to what they see on television. They do not have the luxury of patronizing reality" (110–11). Salutary though such words are, they aren't much help to the even smaller, self-educated segment of that rich part of the world, those viewers who wish to deprovincialize themselves. Given the spectacle, this fit though few must wonder, what is the reality here? How can we possibly know?

The short answer is we can't. We have to do our homework and then make our best guess. What alternative is there? The vast majority of citizens of this country, despite the fact that we are presently conducting two wars (and are engaged in some capacity in numerous additional conflicts), find and feel themselves in the position of external observer, not that of active participant. Yes, we voted for this government (or not), and yes we pay our taxes (or not), but such levels of responsibility and engagement don't compare to that of the soldiers themselves or their families. Meanwhile, the daily experience of life in the countries where these wars are being waged is rarely even dreamed of. And yet, were there world enough and time, some of us—including many unlikely ever to see the shelling or its consequences any place other than on our screens—would prove ourselves conscientious. We keep our eyes open; we want to know the truth. In a mediated world, what this comes down to is: we want to know whom to trust.

But we also need good study aids, and Sontag's diatribe doesn't help. Her beef with the Baudrillards, Debords, and their lesser legions is, in essence, the feel-good flipside of Stephen Colbert's campaign against

Wikipedial truthiness. For Colbert, people today are suckers for good stories. It doesn't have to be true, it just has to sound right. Sontag suggests just the opposite; for her, the ultimate effect of seeing the world from a distance is that it doesn't weigh on us at all. Unlike Atlas, we can just shrug it off. "What can you do?" we think to ourselves, or "It's all just a pack of lies"—and then we go on with business as usual.

I don't believe that we are helpless, nor do I believe that the public is as complacent as Sontag's screed and Colbert's comedy suggest. When we laugh about the prevalence of "truthiness" or we rant about the provinciality of our opinion-makers, we implicitly identify ourselves as different— we see ourselves far from this maddened crowd, and more like Colbert or Sontag. That's why we like them. Writing about representation is self-contradictory, and self-defeating, whenever it encourages the belief that everything is representation.

There exist, of course, alternatives to the thin history of daily newspapers, and to the slick stories of government press offices. For example, a group of more than two hundred professional historians, during the past few years, worked in teams to write a consensus history of the wars of the former Yugoslavia. One way of summing up "The Scholars' Initiative" would be simply to note the project's intention to refute the quotation from Simo Drljača which serves as its epigraph: "You have your facts. We have our facts. You have a complete right to choose between the two versions."[2]

Drljača was instrumental in establishing a series of notorious prison camps near Prijedor in Bosnia-Herzegovina; he himself was killed during an arrest attempt before he could be brought to trial at the International Criminal Tribunal for the Former Yugoslavia (ICTY) in the Hague. Roughly a month after the takeover of Prijedor by Serb forces at the end of April 1992, the three camps of Keraterm, Omarska, and Trnopolje were set up in order to contain the non-Serb male population forced from the city and surrounding villages. In early August, a group of mostly British journalists (representing the *Guardian*, *Newsday*, and the ITN television network) was allowed to visit the camps. Video filmed at Trnopolje, where conditions were somewhat less severe, provoked an international media firestorm. Cameras were not allowed at the other two camps.

Here, from a press release, is an excerpt from the International

Cover of *Time*, August 17, 1992, Trnopolje, Bosnia-Herzegovina.

Criminal Tribunal for the Former Yugoslavia's verdict about the crimes at the camps[3]:

> Like Trnopolje and Keraterm, Omarska camp was officially established on 30 May 1992 by Simo Drljaca [. . .] Planned initially to

function for a fortnight, it in fact remained in operation until 20 August 1992. During this period of almost three months, more than 3,334 detainees at least passed through the camp [. . .] All those detained were interrogated. Almost all were beaten. Many would not leave the camp alive.

The living conditions in Omarska camp were appalling. Some of you, perhaps, remember the images filmed by a television team showing emaciated men, with haggard faces and often a look of resignation or complete dejection. These are the images which would make the international community react and are, perhaps, one of the reasons the Tribunal was established.[4]

In some sense, the very existence of institutions such as the ICTY, and not only their verdicts, refute the simple-minded, militant relativism of the world's Drljačas. Although courts, like historians, are hardly infallible, whatever power they have they are granted.

It may seem striking that the judge of an international court should attribute his mandate to the so-called CNN effect. In this case, however, the tribunal verdict may also be read as an attempt to put an end to the controversy surrounding the media coverage of the Serb-run prison camps. Even Judge Almiro Rodrigues, as he sentenced five participants in the "hellish orgy of persecution" at the camps, likely felt it necessary to respond explicitly to an essay titled "The Picture That Fooled the World," originally published in February 1997 in a journal called *Living Marxism* or LM. The LM essay offered a rather slick (and not entirely unwarranted) critique of the tabloid media's response to the revelation of war crimes at the camps; by doing so, however, its author also attempted to cast doubt on the criminal nature of the camps. Journalists may write the first draft of history, but they don't have the power to issue historical judgments. Judges of war crimes tribunals do.

As the LM essay begins, its author, Thomas Deichmann, makes a claim similar to the one that introduced the Ron Haviv photo exhibition in New York discussed in chapter 2. Commenting on the widely circulated images of emaciated prisoners behind barbed wire (taken by British ITN television at the Trnopolje camp), Deichmann notes: "None of the reporters present in August 1992 described Trnopolje as a concentration camp comparable with Auschwitz. But pictures speak for themselves. The general public around the world that was confronted with this ITN-picture interpreted it without waiting for an explanation."

Of course, even a cursory glance at the photo posted along with Deichmann's own article shows that there was no need for his public to wait for an explanation: as with the cover of *Time*, explanatory words are presented alongside the image. In Deichmann's article, a still from the video footage was posted with a supratitle, and the latter, not the image, is meant to do the talking. (The photo also places a more fully clothed man in the center of the frame, with the more emaciated figures beside and behind him.) This supratitle reads: "The photo that fooled the world." The essay then offers a brief statement, as well as a long list of descriptive claims about the camp (offered without substantiation or references of any kind):

> Now, four and a half years later, it turns out that the media, politics [sic], and the public have been deceived with this picture. It is a proven fact that it is not the group of Muslim men with Fikret Alic that are surrounded by barbed wire, but rather the British reporters. They were standing on a lot to the south of the camp. As a preventive measure against thieves, this lot was surrounded with barbed wire before the war [. . .] There was no barbed-wire fence around the camp area, which also included a school, a community center, and a large open area with a sports field. This was verified by international institutions such as the International Criminal Tribunal in the Hague and the International Red Cross in Geneva. The fact that it was the reporters that were surrounded by barbed wire can be seen in the other film-material that was not edited or broadcasted.

The essential rhetorical move here is familiar to even amateur magicians: if you want to dazzle them, you have to do so by misdirection. Deichmann displaces an argument about events in the world—the prison camps as sites of war crimes—into a dispute over barbed wire and representation.[5] (His veiled suggestion that the prisoners in Trnopolje went to school, played sports, and formed a community is just icing on the cake.) Of course, the ITN footage was edited, cropped, and captioned with a purpose; this was done by everyone—by the TV station itself, by Deichmann, and by the global media coverage that he caricatures. Yet nothing editors, producers, journalists, or photographers do, at least when they are acting as editors, producers, journalists or photographers, creates the events they portray (RIP, Baudrillard).[6]

When I first gave materials discussing these camps to students as part of a War Stories course, my idea was simply to "teach the conflicts." Given that the semester had already provided several occasions for examining the use and abuse of war photos, I felt that Deichmann's article would offer an important cautionary tale. What I myself read as a relatively sophisticated, and sophistic, attempt, in a Bosnian context, to disseminate the equivalent of Holocaust denial was meant as a window into history in the making—a case where the verdict of historians (and, at that point, the ICTY) hadn't yet been delivered.

There are no doubt a number of reasons why my students believed Deichmann, and why they discounted, or didn't read, the other evidence they were given (including coverage of ITN's libel case against *Living Marxism*, which ITN won). Perhaps students invariably trust whatever is given to them on a course syllabus. Yet their response may also suggest that there is an obverse side to the truthiness factor. Today campaigns to discredit the media are at least as powerful, and no doubt easier to mount, than successful propaganda. Rather than a Colbertian state of all-too-easily suspended disbelief, at present we may find ourselves trapped in a supersaturated suspension of particulate histories—ready to believe, or not, whenever the right mix comes together.

The sociologist of science Bruno Latour was right: it is time for critics to stop fighting the last war. As he recently put it, "entire Ph.D. programs are still running to make sure that good American kids are learning the hard way that facts are made up, [. . .] that we are always prisoners of language, that we always speak from a particular standpoint, and so on, while dangerous extremists are using the very same argument [. . .] to destroy hard-won evidence that could save our lives" ("Why Has Critique Run Out of Steam?" 227). Latour goes on to remind us that the best critic is not "the one who debunks, but the one who assembles"—that the "question was never to get *away* from facts but *closer* to them, not fighting empiricism but, on the contrary, renewing empiricism" (246).

If it is to serve any purpose at all, an examination of war stories needs to offer suggestions on how to decipher their language. What, after all, makes one account sound right and another not? Is "sounding right," first and foremost, due simply to our preconceptions? Isn't it also a question of form? Deichmann's misdirection may, paradoxically, perform a valuable service; by encouraging a focus on the effectiveness of his fictions, his article forces us to think about the claim that narrative representations have on reality. What is at stake, in a study of war stories, is the following: if we learn the rules of the game, we may also locate criteria that fine-tune our ears and help identify those accounts most likely to be trustworthy.

In the first of his *Memos for the Next Millennium*, a work that would sum up and conclude his forty years as an author, Italo Calvino offered a similar analysis of the relation between myth and history. Although better known for postmodern metafiction, the Italian writer began his career as a neo-realist, during the aftermath of World War II. The preface to his first novel, an introduction Calvino wrote nearly twenty years after the work itself, reflects on that heady postwar period:

> Having emerged from a [common] experience, a war and a civil war that had spared no one, made communication between the writer and his audience immediate. We were face to face, equals, filled with stories to tell; each had his own [. . .] With our renewed freedom of speech, all at first felt a rage to narrate [. . .] every passenger [. . .] every customer [. . .] every woman waiting in line [. . .] The grayness of daily life seemed to belong to other periods; we moved in a vari-colored universe of stories. (v–vi)

Calvino went on to caution, however, that "the secret of how one wrote then did not lie only in this elementary universality of content." "On the contrary," he remarked, "it had never been so clear that the stories were raw material [. . .] Though we were supposed to be concerned with content, there were never more dogged formalists than we; and never were lyric poets as effusive as [we, supposedly] objective reporters" (vi–vii). And, he concluded, "Actually the extraliterary elements stood there so massive and so indisputable that they seemed a fact of nature; to us the whole problem was one of poetics; how to transform into a literary work that world which for us was the world" (vii). In short, despite the fact that the Italian neorealists, even today, are still portrayed as "objective report-ers," Calvino emphasized that theirs was a search for a form of storytell-ing equal to their war experience. Existing forms, they must have felt, were inadequate for the task at hand.

Twenty years later still, and forty years after his postwar novel, Calvino would begin his first memo for the next millennium by defining his life-long literary practice. "My working method," he remarked, "has more often than not involved *the subtraction of weight*"; his aim in this initial lec-ture, he added, was to explain "why I have come to consider *lightness* a value rather than a defect" (3, my emphasis). As a first example of weight, the Italian novelist returned once again to his earliest stories, noting that, during those same postwar years "the categorical imperative of every young writer was to represent" what he described as "the ruthless ener-gies propelling the events of our century" (3). For the young Calvino, this imperative became increasingly burdensome:

> Soon I became aware that between the facts of life that should have been my raw materials and the quick light touch I wanted for my writing, there was a gulf that cost me increasing effort to cross. Maybe I was only then becoming aware of the weight, the inertia, the opacity of the world [. . .]
>
> At certain moments I felt that the entire world was turning to stone: a slow petrification, more or less advanced depending on people and places but one that spared no aspect of life. It was as if no one could escape the inexorable stare of Medusa. (4)

Bringing these remarks into the present discussion is meant to empha-size what the Italian author's language obscures: what Calvino refers to in his memo as "the frantic spectacle of the world" is never named directly. It goes literally without saying that those weighty "facts of life," "the events of our century," are—still and again—a "war and civil war that had spared no one."

In a word, the weight Calvino carried, and kept in the bag, was the war. All the more important, then, to note that this inaugural "memo" really takes off only in the paragraphs that follow—with his retelling of a Greek myth, the story of the warrior Perseus, of his winged sandals and his polished bronze shield. "Thus," the writer himself comments, "Perseus comes to my aid [. . .] just as I too am about to be caught in a vise of stone—which happens every time I try to speak about my own past" (4). He then emphasizes the relevance of this myth to his general theme:

> To cut off Medusa's head without being turned to stone, Perseus
> supports himself on the very lightest of things, the winds and the
> clouds, and fixes his gaze upon what can be revealed only by indirect
> vision, an image caught in a mirror. I am immediately tempted to see
> this myth as an allegory on the poet's relationship to the world, a
> lesson in the method to follow when writing. (4)

The warrior's story, of course, does not end there. Perseus goes on to establish the very paradigm of heroism: he frees a princess, Andromeda, from her chains and slays a sea-monster with his sword. "As for the severed head [of Medusa,]" Calvino reminds us, "Perseus does not abandon it but carries it concealed in a bag. When his enemies are about to overcome him, he has only to display it, holding it by its snaky locks, and this bloodstained booty becomes an invincible weapon in the hero's hand" (5). In concluding, the Italian author draws another parallel between myth and history:

> Perseus succeeds in mastering that horrendous face by keeping it
> hidden, just as in the first place he vanquished it by viewing it in a
> mirror. Perseus's strength lies in his insistent refusal to look directly,
> but never in a refusal of the reality in which he is fated to live; he car-
> ries that reality with him and accepts it as his particular burden. (5)

As his 1964 preface makes clear, Calvino came to believe that his early neorealist writing was created as much by history as by himself; like Perseus, the strength of the postmodern Calvino would lie in his "refusal to look directly, but not in a refusal of reality itself," a reality that continued to be his "particular burden." One would not be far off, in short, in surmising that this reading of the Greek myth illustrates Calvino's own solution to the problem of poetics which first faced him during the postwar years, the question of "how to transform into a literary work that world which for [him] was the world." Perseus thus offers a lesson concerning the method Calvino himself followed when writing, from the postwar years until his death in 1985, the year the lecture on lightness was written.

So how are we to understand that method, and how might it help us parse the barrage of war images and stories which assault our screens daily? First of all, Calvino emphasizes the truth of fiction. As retold by the Italian fabulist, the Perseus myth suggests that war stories have powers of their own. The image reflected in the shield is an emblem of strength, even conquest; category difference here is no defect, nor does it leave the world behind. On the contrary, the image in polished bronze is the sole means of bridging the gulf, of completing the quest. As he concludes, Calvino stresses this point, noting that he is "accustomed to consider literature a search for knowledge." Indeed, he thinks of language use itself as a sort of ongoing epistemological tribunal, "as a perpetual pursuit of things, as a perpetual adjustment to their infinite variety" (26).

Opposed to Calvino, there is Deichmann, a propagandist masquerading as an objective observer, as a revealer of facts. For Calvino, any writing of that sort, *true or not*, any writing that purports to transmit information rather than pursue knowledge is petrified speech, as deadly as it is weighty. Deichmann claims to unveil a truth long hidden from his readers; he pulls it out of the bag and thrusts it in their faces. Rather than search for knowledge, Deichmann locks onto petrified certitude; the very term he uses to describe it—"proven fact"—is redundant, it protests too much. Calvino, in contrast, teaches us that the converse of the Socratic dictum is also true. The Greek philosopher famously said that his only claim to wisdom consisted in that, unlike others, he knew he knew nothing. When it comes to representing war, he who doesn't know that he doesn't know is a fool.[7]

Yet at least these facts are clear, we tell ourselves. Early on the morning of May 16, 1968, the soldiers of Charlie Company entered the small village of My Lai, in the Quang Ngai province of Vietnam. By noon there would hardly be a village. At least 343 people were killed, perhaps more than 500. After the massacre, a U.S. soldier reported that "they hadn't seen one military-age male in the place." Tim O'Brien describes it this way:

"They met no resistance. No enemy. No incoming fire. Still, for the next four hours, Charlie Company killed whatever could be killed. They killed chickens. They killed dogs and cattle. They killed people, too. Lots of people. Women, infants, teen-agers, old men" ("The Vietnam in Me" 233). A photo taken that morning would later be used as a poster for the antiwar movement. Transcribed on it, in red ink above and below the slaughtered Vietnamese, was a brief exchange between the 60 Minutes anchor Mike Wallace and Paul Meadlo, a soldier from Charlie Company. "Q. And babies? A. And babies."

"Absolute occurrence is irrelevant." Tim O'Brien said that too, in one of his most famous stories. The title of this tale from The Things They Carried—"How to Tell a True War Story"—is borrowed from the language of cookbooks, or repair manuals: the author promises instructions, perhaps even colorful illustrations of the results. The phrase also plays on the double meaning of the verb "to tell": how to tell a story truly, but also how to tell truth from lies. In other words, O'Brien offers illustrations of storytelling form, but he also shows us which storytellers to trust.

Toward the end of this text, O'Brien riffs on a war story cliché to illustrate a paradox. Some war stories are not true, he claims, even if the events they describe actually happened, and others may never have happened, yet are still true: "Absolute occurrence is irrelevant" (83). Take that old chestnut about a guy throwing himself on a grenade to save his buddies, says O'Brien; that one might even have happened (stranger things have), but mere happening wouldn't make it true. A "true war story," he comments, "doesn't depend on that kind of truth" (83). O'Brien then offers his own, never-really-happened-but-still-true version of this scene: "Four guys go down a trail. A grenade sails out. One guy jumps on it and takes the blast, but it's a killer grenade and everybody dies anyway. Before they die, though, one of the dead guys says, 'The fuck you do that for?' and the jumper says, 'Story of my life, man,' and the other guy starts to smile but he's dead" (83–84).

So what makes this story true? Rewriting a formulaic image of heroism, O'Brien emphasizes the cliché's hubris, that arrogance about one's ability to control events, bound to fall sooner or later. His revised standard version instead cuts to the chase and focuses on the fall; its truth is seen even by the dead guys. What makes this story true is not whether it happened, but that it *always* happens. "Story of my life, man." Story time is mythic time: a singular event is taken as emblem, a representation of the way of the world.

Seen in this light, the effectiveness of Deichmann's barbed wire ploy becomes easier to explain. In essence, there are two competing narratives at work: first, that of concentration camps, and second, that of media manipulation. The impact of either, much like that of O'Brien's story, is grounded in the observer's sense of what "always happens." Deichmann aims to displace one subtext—"it's happening again, the Nazis are back"—with another, one that is much less disquieting: "no, they're just lying to us, like they always do." Who wouldn't prefer the second scenario to the horror of the first? Moreover, though both narratives make claims about "the facts on the ground," they do so by mobilizing stories that are formally distinct: a gothic tale of horror competes with a muckraker's crusade. Neither story requires, it should be stressed, an adult audience.

For many years, one of the most intriguing figures to traverse the unmapped minefields between fiction and document has been the filmmaker Errol Morris. The pages of his *New York Times* blog have recently addressed the issue of photographic truth directly, generally taking up the cause of photographers against those who would malign them. Morris's own position is clear:

> Photographs are neither true nor false in and of themselves. They are only true and false with respect to statements that we make about them or the questions that we might ask of them. The photograph doesn't give me answers. A lot of additional investigation could provide those answers, but who has time for that?
>
> Pictures may be worth a thousand words, but there are two words that you can never apply to them: "true" and "false." ("Liar, Liar, Pants on Fire")

When Morris asks "who has time for that?," the question appears to be rhetorical, yet a three-part series of essays on that same blog demonstrates that, in one particular case, Morris himself did find the time.

Writing about a pair of famous Crimean war photos by Roger Fenton, the filmmaker would expend roughly twenty-five thousand words and travel over five thousand miles.

Fenton took two shots from the same location of a desolate, battle-scarred landscape, a site that had been nicknamed by soldiers "The Valley of Death." In one shot, cannonballs are scattered across the road; in the other, there are no cannonballs on the road, and more cannonballs are found along the roadside. A number of critics have assumed that Fenton staged the photo Morris refers to as "ON," either by having the cannon-balls placed on the road or by doing it himself. As Morris argues, such a reading assumes an order between the two shots (first "OFF," then "ON") so as to tell a story about the photographer and his method. Couldn't the sequence, he asks, have actually been the reverse?

The filmmaker cites Sontag's *Regarding the Pain of Others* as the inspira-tion for his Crimean quest. The relevant pages of that work, however, also reference other controversies from the history of war photography, includ-ing one involving the Civil War photographers associated with Mathew Brady. A photograph by Timothy O'Sullivan, taken in the aftermath of Gettysburg, may well be the single most famous shot of the battlefield dead. This celebrated photo, however, also carries the taint of fraud, fol-lowing a study of the Brady studio photographers by William Frassanito. Matching details within this image to another photo, taken by O'Sullivan and also printed in Alexander Gardner's two-volume *Photographic Sketch Book of the War* (published in 1865 and 1866), Frassanito concluded that the first photo reprinted here on top titled by Gardner "Incidents of the War. A Harvest of Death," shows the same dead soldiers as the other, though the location of the camera was different.

The problems don't stop there. In Gardner's description of this second photo, which he calls "Field Where General Reynolds Fell. Battlefield of Gettysburg," the dead are identified as Union soldiers; in his description of the first photo, they were said to be Confederate. Here Morris's dictum seems useful, even essential; surely it is the claims made about these pho-tos which must be judged as true or false, not the photos themselves.

An even more troubling accusation by Frassanito, however, involves another sequence of photographs, and only one dead soldier—although here it appears that more than the camera was moved. The case is sum-

Valley of the Shadow of Death. Photographs by Roger Fenton, 1855. Harry Ransom Center, University of Texas, Austin.

Top: "Incidents of the War. A Harvest of Death," Gettysburg, Pa., July, 1863. Photographed by Timothy H. O'Sullivan, July 1863. Library of Congress, Prints and Photographs Division, LC-B8184-7964-A. *Bottom:* Gettysburg, Pa., Bodies of Federal soldiers, killed on July 1, near the McPherson woods. Photographed by Timothy H. O'Sullivan, July 1863. Library of Congress, Prints and Photographs Division, LC-B8171-0234.

marized in a discussion on the Library of Congress American Memory website:[8]

> Frassanito studied six photographs of this dead soldier made by the photographers Alexander Gardner and Timothy O'Sullivan at the Gettysburg battlefield in July 1863. Geographic features place four of the six photographs at the southern slope of Devil's Den and two at what Gardner called the "sharpshooter's den." Frassanito argues that the original location of the body was the southern slope of Devil's Den, suggesting that the soldier was probably an infantryman, killed while advancing up the hillside. After taking pictures of the dead soldier from several angles, the two photographers noticed the picturesque sharpshooter's den—forty yards away—and moved the corpse to this rocky niche and photographed him again. A blanket, visible under the soldier in another version of the sharpshooter's den image [. . .] may have been used to carry the body.

The website commentary notes as well that

> the type of weapon seen in these photographs was not used by sharpshooters. This particular firearm is seen in a number of Gardner's scenes at Gettysburg and probably was the photographer's prop. The amount of time expended photographing this one body indicates that this may have been one of the last bodies to be buried and Gardner may have felt that he was running out of subjects.

Like Roger Fenton in the controversy analyzed by Morris, Gardner and O'Sullivan stand accused of rearranging the elements of their photographs and, by extension, of lying to their public. If Frassanito's analysis is correct, the case against the Civil War photographers does seem damning: the content of images was mislabeled and paired with misleading, even fictional commentary; moreover, the photographers didn't hesitate to insert props into their shots and even pose the dead in "artistic" positions or places.

Although these three cases of alleged trickery bear a certain resemblance, I strongly suspect that most people react to them quite differently. In fact, my guess is that the general level of outrage escalates in response to each. Had Frassanito published in the nineteenth century, not the twentieth, I imagine

Top: Gettysburg, Pa., Dead Confederate soldiers in "the devil's den." Photographed by Alexander Gardner, July 1863. Library of Congress, Prints and Photographs Division, LC-B8171-0277. Bottom: Gettysburg, Pa., Dead Confederate soldier in "the devil's den." Photographed by Alexander Gardner, July 1863. Library of Congress, Prints and Photographs Division, LC-B8171-7942.

that the reaction would have been: (1) "Fenton wants to move a few cannon-balls? Doesn't seem right to me, but, well, they're just cannonballs"; (2) "What do you mean those corpses aren't the enemy's dead? Good Lord, do those photographers have no shame!?!"; and (3) "They did what?!! They moved the dead soldier's body?!! For a picture?!! They should be put in jail!!!"

In short, our response to this sort of chicanery is based only in part on our sense that the photographs falsify their subject. Most important is the subject itself. The representation of war, by definition, opens up moral concerns. And, as recent research in neuroscience suggests, different kinds of moral issues affect us in very different ways.

Joshua Greene, a professor in the psychology department at Harvard University, studies the interplay between emotional and analytic processes in moral judgment; he has found that separate areas of the brain become active when experimental subjects confront two contrasting sorts of moral dilemmas. Using functional magnetic resonance imaging (fMRI) technology, which maps blood flow to the brain, Greene asked his subjects how they would act, given the following scenario:

> "A runaway trolley is headed for five people who will be killed if it proceeds on its present course. The only way to save them is to hit a switch that will divert the trolley onto an alternate set of tracks where it will kill one person instead of five. Ought you to turn [sic] the trolley in order to save five people at the expense of one?" ("An fMRI Investigation" 2105)

What would you do? According to Greene, about nine out of ten people say yes.

> "Now consider a similar problem, the footbridge dilemma. As before, a trolley threatens to kill five people. You are standing next to a large stranger on a footbridge that spans the tracks, in between the oncoming trolley and the five people. In this scenario, the only way to save the five people is to push this stranger off the bridge, onto the tracks below. He will die if you do this, but his body will stop the trolley from reaching the others. Ought you to save the five others by pushing this stranger to his death?" (Ibid.)

Again, what do you think? Here, once again, the results—across age, gender, race, or what have you—are just as striking. Except they're the reverse. Nine out of ten say no.

Under an fMRI scan, different parts of the brain light up while we're making our choices. It appears that, in order to make such decisions, the brain utilizes different systems that do different things, one for moral calculations, another that is more emotional—it simply doesn't like killing. The struggle between the two, Greene suspects, is what determines our moral behavior. Greene attributes the emotive side of moralizing to eons of evolution; the utilitarian, calculating form of morality is much more recent. Thus, he comments, whereas "basic primate morality"—our "inner chimp"—doesn't understand tax evasion, it does get "pushing your buddy off a cliff" (Abumrad and Krulwich). In WNYC's Radiolab discussion of Greene's research, reporter Robert Krulwich suggests that the competition between different brain areas seems like a sort of "bleacher morality"—as if whichever side manages to shout louder wins.

As it turns out, the real story is probably even more complex: the shouting match may have a referee. Both of the problems presented above are similar insofar as our responses seem clear-cut, almost intuitive. Yet people overwhelmingly make choices that are logical opposites: they pull the level, but they refuse to push the guy off the bridge. In another experiment, Greene has interrogated his subjects using a third scenario, one similar to the final episode of the TV show M.A.S.H. Faced with this particular dilemma, people generally have a much more difficult time making up their minds:

> Enemy soldiers have taken over your village. They have orders to kill all remaining civilians. You and some of your townspeople have sought refuge in the cellar of a large house. Outside, you hear the voices of soldiers who have come to search the house for valuables.
>
> Your baby begins to cry loudly. You cover his mouth to block the sound. If you remove your hand from his mouth, his crying will summon the attention of the soldiers who will kill you, your child, and the others hiding out in the cellar. To save yourself and the others, you must smother your child to death.
>
> Is it appropriate for you to smother your child in order to save yourself and the other townspeople? (Greene, "Neural Bases" 390)

In this case, as it turns out, the results are roughly equal: half envision killing their baby, and half cannot. In close contests like this, according to Greene, additional brain areas become active, specifically those involved with response conflict and cognitive control. The latter area tends to light up when subjects decide that the best overall consequences are indeed paramount. In other words, according to Greene, when people say, "Yes, it's okay to smother the baby," they exhibit increased activity in parts of the brain associated with high-level cognitive function. The end result of such activity apparently boosts our moral calculator and dampens our inner chimp.

If you've followed this chapter's peregrinations thus far, you may be wondering just where we're wandering . . . and why. Postmodern pedants, a Greek myth, Bosnian prison camps, a killer story about a grenade, early war photography's greatest hits, and now a murderous trolley car: each of these sundry examples offers evidence for the power of fiction. It is no coincidence that in today's world business executives study Dante and returning veterans work through Homer: narrative constructions, fictive or non-, make meaning from history and call it truth. Note that, to test his theories about moral decisionmaking, the neuroscientist Joshua Greene also borrows stories, some from philosophers, another from a popular television show. To explain the composition of celebrated war photographs, historians and museum curators reconstruct events and imagine motives, and they too become storytellers. To counter a report of concentration camp horrors, an accusation of scandal is made, as if the second story trumps the first. And so on, and so forth.

So where is the real in all of this? First, it ought to be clear that imaginary tales, when properly told, have very real effects. Even though we are, in a literal sense, playing with tokens, empathic participation in a wartime drama about crying babies, just like a photo shoot that involves dragging around dead bodies, can cause real revulsion. Our examination of these stories is intended to bring us closer to those events, to help us to understand them as they were experienced by those directly involved. For this very reason, though I certainly don't recommend smothering babies or moving corpses, I do think we owe Alexander Gardner a more complete hearing.

   The short essays accompanying the Brady studio's photos in Gardner's *Photographic Sketch Book* were written for the winners. It is no coincidence, for example, that the annotations regarding the scenes of slaughter presented in the pair of Gettysburg images identify the soldiers in the first photo as Confederate. The horrific grimace at the center of the frame appears to distill the violence that scattered these bodies like ragdolls, yet this expression contrasts sharply with the faces seen in the second photo—faces identified as Union. Gardner's commentaries call attention to these very details. In annotating the first photo ("Harvest of Death"), the artist notes that

> a battle has been often the subject of elaborate description; but it can be described in one simple word, *devilish!* and the distorted dead recall the ancient legends of men torn in pieces by the savage wantonness of fiends. Swept down without preparation, the shattered bodies fall in all conceivable positions.

Describing the next plate, Gardner takes an opposite tack. He instead recalls for his readers that, on the battlefield,

> some of the dead presented an aspect which showed that they had suffered severely just previous to dissolution, but these were few in number compared with those who wore a calm and resigned expression, as though they had passed away in the act of prayer. Others had a smile on their faces, and looked as if they were in the act of speaking.

Attempting to comfort, this description closes with a portrait of the battlefield as a monumental, yet pastoral scene, the perfect Victorian cemetery:

> The faces of all were pale, as though cut in marble, and as the wind swept across the battle-field it waved the hair, and gave the bodies such an appearance of life that a spectator could hardly help thinking they were about to rise to continue the fight.

In sharp contrast to his previous description, Gardner's vision of near-resurrection is heavenly rather than devilish; it is also in harmony with the sentiment that "we can not dedicate—we can not consecrate—we can not hallow—this ground," that the "brave men, living and dead, who struggled here, have consecrated it, far above our poor power to add or detract."

A few pages later, in his description of the second sharpshooter photo, the photographer makes explicit reference to the dedication of the National Cemetery at Gettysburg. Gardner notes that he attended those ceremonies on November 19, 1863 (where Lincoln's address, in a brief two minutes, accomplished what the renowned orator Edward Everett had attempted for over two hours). After the pomp and circumstance had ended, the photographer ostensibly decided to visit again the "Sharp-shooter's Home." In what is almost certainly a work of pure fiction, Gardner describes the site that day:

> The musket, rusted by many storms, still leaned against the rock, and the skeleton of the soldier lay undisturbed within the moulder-ing uniform, as did the cold form of the dead four months before. None of those who went up and down the fields to bury the fallen, had found him. "Missing," was all that could have been known of him at home, and some mother may yet be patiently watching for the return of her boy, whose bones lie bleaching, unrecognized and alone, between the rocks at Gettysburg.

Like his title for the previous plate ("A Sharpshooter's Last Sleep"), Gardner's language here is insistently sentimental. The image of a patient, helpless, grieving mother is contrasted with the bones that still lie bleaching; in his description on the page before, the photographer had already set up this sentimental tableau:

> How many skeletons of such men are bleaching to-day in out of the way places no one can tell. Now and then the visitor to a battle-field finds the bones of some man shot as this one was, but there are hun-dreds that will never be known of, and will moulder into nothing-ness among the rocks.

The dead soldier's allegiances are not identified in this first passage, he is simply "a sharpshooter." Yet in the second photo, we are told: the dead sniper left unburied, ostensibly for months, was a Confederate soldier. When Gardner tells of his return visit to the site, however, such sectarian concerns are forgotten again—as if all that remains of the war are the remains themselves. Such shifting identifications make it clear that

Gardner's is no stance of neutrality. Like the writings of Whitman, his is an active effort at national reconstruction.

In contrast, the discomfort of modern readers at the manipulations used to create these early war photographs does assume that neutrality is possible; implicitly, such a reaction places the camera as a neutral, scientific observer. Like Rousseau's imprisoned man, we trap the photographer behind his lens; if he puts the camera down, even to caption his own photos, the photographer becomes something other than a photographer. And if he does not put it down, our discomfort with him actually increases; how often, we wonder, has this chronicler of war kept on shooting when he ought to have intervened? Do war photographers simply pull the lever, or do they push the man from the bridge? Or perhaps we resent these photographers because their photos reveal something about us— that we also share Rousseau's prison. Are we helpless? Do we intervene?

More problematic still, Gardner's descriptions serve to displace our focus on events in the world onto his representation of those events. In this they are no different from Deichmann's. It is as if the photographer tells us that the truth of war is in his photographs, not in the world ("Absolute occurrence is irrelevant"). In this case, however, unlike Deichmann, the photographer may have been right. Although the sentimentality of Gardner's narratives is today hard to miss, echoes in them of more famous and more lasting words, those of Whitman and Lincoln, are undeniable as well. By the time the photographer published his collection of plates, both our national poet and our martyred president had already envisioned a mythic Union, one grounded in nameless, nationalized sacrifice, and they did so after "a war and civil war that had spared no one." For Alexander Gardner, the images reflected in his industrial-age equivalent of a bronze shield captured a battlefield where the anonymous dead still lay, and over which mothers still grieved. Although his descriptions of those images have long since turned to stone, funereal monuments do have their place in our histories, in our hills and fields, and in our lives.

In April 1990, the historian Saul Friedlander organized a conference at the University of California, Los Angeles, called "Probing the Limits of Representation: Nazism and the 'Final Solution.'" The central figure at this academic event, apart from the convener himself, was the theorist Hayden White. Richard Wetzell, in his review of the conference proceedings, summarizes both White's "proposition that all historical narratives draw on generic story patterns—such as epic, tragedy, comedy—to fashion historical facts into a 'story' " and his conclusion that " 'there are no grounds to be found in the historical record itself for preferring one way of construing its meaning over another.' " Wetzell then comments, "It is easy to see that the relativist implications of this statement might be regarded as especially troubling when one is dealing with the Holocaust" (87).[9] Given that Friedlander himself had recently written a powerful "indictment of histories, novels, and films that, under the guise of seeming to portray faithfully [. . .] actually aestheticize the whole scene and translate its contents into fetish objects and the stuff of sadomasochistic fantasies" (White 30–31), it is equally easy to see why the historian might have wanted to confront the theorist in person.

The relevance of this controversy to the present chapter should be apparent as well. Our questions about how to parse the myriad representations of war are also White's questions. In his UCLA address, Hayden White rose to the challenge laid down for him by Friedlander: he argued that a specific form of writing, that typical of literary modernism, is best suited for Holocaust representation, using a text by the Italian modernist and Holocaust survivor Primo Levi to close his remarks. Rather than rehearse these arguments here, I instead follow White's example and end this chapter with a war story that I myself find unimpeachable, arguing that, in the case of the recent conflict in Bosnia, the real war got into a comic book.

Joe Sacco's *Safe Area Goražde* was the second of his book-length works to use a graphic novel format as a vehicle for traditional investigative journalism. The first, *Palestine*, is an equally devastating read but less consistent in form, as if the author was still honing the tools of his storytelling trade. *Goražde*, in contrast, is self-reflexive in the extreme as it attempts to match representational form to historical context. A quick look at his opening chapter illustrates this point.

From the opening pages, Sacco's readers will be struck by the detail of his artwork; the drawing could be called realistic in the conventional

Safe Area Goražde, Chapter 1, "Go Away"

sense, although the human figures are somewhat more iconic, more "cartoony," than the world they inhabit. This stylistic choice unifies the book as a whole. Sacco clearly came to Bosnia armed with a camera and tape recorder, not a sword, winged sandals, and a shield. His book also opens with an approach to his subject which is absolutely literal. As we turn these early pages, however, we begin to see variety in both perspective and in panel size. The former is more varied than the latter: there are a number of long, establishing shots, panoramas, but we also follow the children, perhaps even seeing the world through their eyes, as a UN convoy slowly makes its way in the city.

Sacco makes that arrival—which was his arrival as well—coincide with our own readerly emplacement into the scene of narration. As such, he pairs his experience with ours. This choice frames his narrative as a whole; the story concludes with Sacco's final departure from Goražde, days after the agreement that ended the war was signed.

So far I haven't said anything about the history that his admirably succinct exposition engages. The narrator's commentary summarizes the events that briefly made the city of Goražde a topic of international concern: a sequence of images shows the UN convoy, first approaching and then entering the city from a variety of angles and a number of different distances.

Only in the chapter's final panel, however, do we see Goražde from the tank's-eye view. The impact of the contrast made explicit in this final image reveals the abyss between the massed crowds of Goraždans in waiting and the protected, limited vision of any talk that trades cities like cards. To draw this scene Sacco had to first learn for himself what it would mean to have an entire city "go away." This is a lesson of Perseidic realism: even the object has a point of view. So don't be ashamed to look it in the face.

Sacco isn't one to forget this lesson, although his work follows Perseus in the usual sense as well: *Safe Area Goražde* offers no direct access, no face-to-face encounter with the war. (One might expect otherwise in a medium in which geopolitical discussions are most often conducted by muscle-bound figures in tights and a cape.) A pair of chapters further on, Sacco makes the mediation explicit, spending several pages showing the reader

It was an enclave. It was surrounded by separatist Serb forces, it had been since the beginning of the Bosnian War more than three and a half years ago. And it was a U.N.-designated safe area...

The two other eastern enclaves, Srebrenica and Zepa, also designated safe areas, had been abandoned by the U.N. in the summer. The victorious Serbs entered Srebrenica and Zepa, and, in the aftermath, horrible stories had emerged...

When British and Ukranian U.N. peace-keepers pulled out of Gorazde shortly thereafter, Gorazdans thought they, too, had been abandoned...

2

Safe Area Goražde, The Convoy Approaches

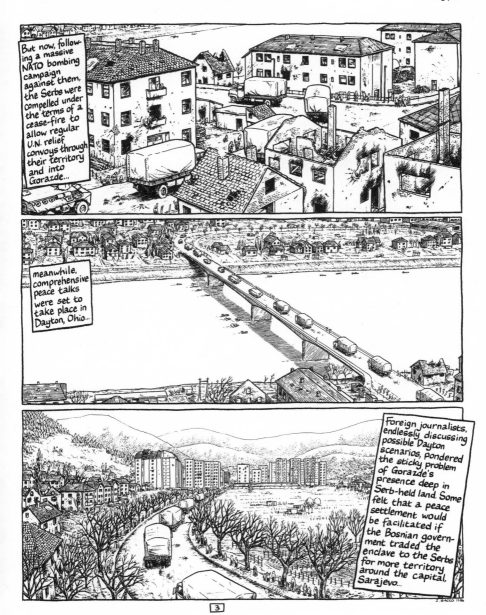

Safe Area Goražde, Views of Goražde

Safe Area Goražde, The Center of Town

Safe Area Goražde, Hanging with Edin.

around Goražde the way he got around—with an interpreter every step of the way (16).

Sacco's key informant, Edin, is foregrounded in much of the text; his stories, his experiences, and thus, by extension, his judgments and values are staged in a variety of ways, including the comic-strip equivalents of

Safe Area Goražde, Maybe There's Peace.

"talking-head" and "voice-over" presentations. As we know from the introduction, Sacco arrived in Goražde at the end of the war, during the weeks between the NATO bombings and the peace talks. As a result, Edin and the numerous other Goraždans in the tale are his only access to the history of the city under siege and to events elsewhere along the Drina. In the flashbacks that tell of these gruesome events, Sacco's representational style doesn't vary—only his interlocutors, and their number, do. With minor exceptions, his sketching of place remains realistic, the people a little less so; the effect is to unify the presentation of past events into the present tense of Sacco's visit.

In terms of the tale it tells, Sacco's *Goražde* is noncontroversial. From its very first chapter, the main story is clearly the lives of Goražde's citizens in wartime, and this reality will be set against larger-scale political events— lived truths that counter dangerous fictions. From the beginning of the Sarajevo siege, this story was the one story that *everyone* told, in newspapers, on TV, through journals, in fiction, on film, everywhere. A short list of titles available to the American market make this clear: *Zlata's Diary*, *Logavina Street*, *Sarajevo Daily*. And, I hasten to add, the media weren't wrong. Civilians in wartime *is* the real story of our time, though you'd never know it by reading the U.S. media on Iraq.

So then, if everyone had this story, why argue that Sacco in particular nailed it? Take another look at the narrator. The contrast between detailed settings and more cartoonish people is complicated somewhat by Sacco's self-portrayal, set explicitly and consistently one cartoonish level above that of all other characters. Behind his whited-out glasses, Sacco's narrator slouches, drips sweat, confesses to hangovers, and embarrasses himself, usually with women. He is also on occasion drawn with fish lips and other exaggerated features. Such self-deflation is effective in gaining the reader's trust, but it stems directly from the Socratic mode of the storytelling. Sacco's wisdom lies in making clear that he knows he doesn't know.

After more than two hundred pages, the conclusion of *Safe Area Goražde* at last recounts the single most significant event that Sacco witnessed (209). The scene portrays couch potatoes à la Bosanski: winter clothing indoors, a smoke-filled room, and television with VCR (powered by a homemade watermill). The event itself is transmitted via the discharge of automatic weaponry, doubtless in response to televised images on CNN; the effect of the shooting is to add one more monitor to the CNN network, a network that brings together, among others, Bosnian Muslims and

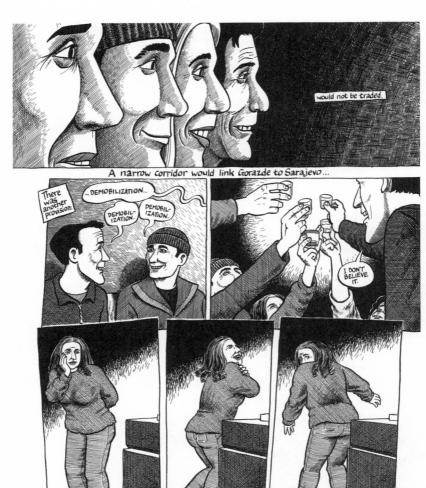

Safe Area Goražde, No Trade.

Bosnian Serbs. By end of the page, we should also note, Sacco himself is no longer in the frame. As every journalism student knows, *he* is not the story.

An event is lived experience, not an agreed-upon fiction. The revolution will not be televised. And although we are not Goraždans, we do,

Safe Area Goražde, Still an Enclave.

owing to Sacco's efforts, have some understanding of the importance of that two-word question, placed outside the frame of every panel on the page. "And Gorazde?" And so we flip hurriedly to the next (210). The question that lingers from the previous page is here completed and transformed into a statement, as Sacco's close-up leaves the television out of the frame. Here again, he leaves himself out as well—only his arm and hand appear, sharing a toast but not showing his face. Which leaves only a victory spiral, to be performed by Dalila solo, although a subsequent panel will portray her beckoning to the television and inviting President Clinton to join her. (As you might recall, in the final months of 1995, he was otherwise occupied.)

And of course it doesn't end there. Rather than turn Sacco into Hollywood, I should leave you with one more page (215). Once again, in the closing pages of the book, a geopolitical perspective is framed by the experience and interpretations of two informants. As Edin comments, the peace accords, as far as Goražde is concerned, leave everything to be done. And without return of refugees, most urgently that of Bosnian Muslims to Goražde's neighboring cities of Foča, Višegrad, and Srebrenica, nothing can be done. Goražde will not be able to continue, except perhaps as an enclave. And cities, as Sacco would be first to remind us, do not "just go away."

The Goraždans Sacco portrays are more than a few souls among Sontag's "hundreds of millions of television watchers who are far from inured to what they see on television." Certainly their story, as told in *Safe Area Goražde*, gives the lie to the more flip theories about our "society of spectacle." And yet narration in this text must still be described as postmodern. If literary modernism, according to White, is the mode best suited to the horrors of World War II,[10] the multiplicity of perspectives that Sacco records, and the uncertain hand that helps us sort among them, are similar insofar as they too are directly opposed to that controlling, authoritative voice most traditionally associated with realism. Yet I still feel that, for history in the making, Sacco's form of witness is as real as it gets.

5

Aggressors
The Beast Is Back

The people were divided into the persecuted and those who persecuted them. That wild beast, which lives in man and does not dare to show itself until the barriers of law and custom have been removed, was now set free. The signal was given, the barriers were down. As has so often happened in the history of man, permission was tacitly granted for acts of violence and plunder, even for murder, if they were carried out in the name of higher interests, according to established rules, and against a limited number of men of a particular type and belief. A man who saw clearly and with open eyes and was then living could see how this miracle took place and how the whole of society could, in a single day, be transformed.

—Ivo Andrić, *Bridge on the Drina*

Nations, and the people who form them, differ in the degree to which their memory of history—and the violence that punctuates it—remains active, generative of their collective identity. In the quotation from Ivo Andrić's *Bridge on the Drina*, no mention is given of a specific historical moment, yet it is hard to imagine a citizen of the former Yugoslavia who would not recognize the passage instantly, and also know that it refers to the horrendous outbreak of the violence during the Second World War. Today, of course, the passage also carries a more contemporary resonance, and it is not surprising that chroniclers of the destruction of Yugoslavia have singled out these lines, implying that Andrić's eloquent words were not simply descriptive but also prophetic. By stripping his prose of historical referents, and by envisioning violence as a "beast within," Andrić created a text that would itself become a territory of struggle, his Nobel Prize a crown that opposing forces would read in ominously different ways.

During the recent Yugoslav wars, World War II was only rarely an abstract metaphor. A poster created by the Ministry of Information of the short-lived Republic of Serbian Krajina, for example, portrays the clinking glasses of a toast, one in the hand of a man with a Croatian nationalist cufflink, the other in that of a demon. Behind the bubbly, revealed by parted curtains, is a Nazi flag. Framing this image are the words "The Beast Is Out Again" (the substantive written, for good measure, in German Gothic script). Not a work of particular subtlety, but then the poster was done in English. In the 1990s, it was apparently felt that an Anglophone audience needed to be reminded that Croats were Nazis, and in league with the devil.

On a different front, early in *The Great War and Modern Memory*, Paul Fussell reminds his readers of how unprepared in 1914 the average Englishman was for the cataclysm about to unfold, or for any war, actually. His subtitle cites Philip Larkin's *MCMXIV*—"Never such innocence again." Fussell adds, "That was a different world. The certainties were intact. Britain had not known a major war for over a century and on the Continent, as A. J. P. Taylor points out, 'there had been no war between the Great Powers since 1871. No man in the prime of his life knew what war was like. All imagined that it would be an affair of great marches and great battles, quickly decided'" (21). As Gertrude Stein famously quipped, the United States had lost its youthful innocence some years earlier; we entered the brutal twentieth century at the beginning of our Civil War. The picnic baskets and lawn chairs that the Washington elite brought to watch Bull Run would be packed up and stowed long before Franz Ferdinand took his one-way trip through the streets of Sarajevo.

When I taught my first War Stories course in the spring of 2003, frankly, U.S. college students didn't seem all that different from the average Briton in the spring of 1914. September 11, the Afghanistan invasion, build-up to the war in Iraq . . . certainly the presence of war was everywhere, but this was definitely not the Vietnam generation. The wars they remembered— vaguely—were distant wars; war itself was a distant, nebulous idea.

And apparently the parents had been taught by their children. How else to explain the response to 9/11? Those flags sprouting up like mushrooms made my foreign students—particularly the Germans—uneasy. Me they reminded of picnic baskets, as if we were all preparing for a sporting event, a tailgating get-together as big as the nation. On the other hand, my first War Stories syllabus might simply have been shaped by its venue. That initial class was at Hampshire College, an alternative-ed school, and the second time through was at Smith, a college for women. For whatever reason, I began the course with an opening section on compassion, and ended it by focusing on war journalism and photojournalism. As if all we'd be doing was observing.

In a world where wars across the globe are screened on our televisions and computers, it would be absurd to argue that Rousseau's compassionate observer belongs to any one nation. Yet there is a peculiarly American fascination with this perspective; the stories we tell ourselves about ourselves fit it rather neatly. Isolationists first, then liberators in two world wars, we have since played the liberation theme over and over again, most notably in Central and South America, most recently in Afghanistan and Iraq. Like Rousseau's onlooker, we anguish over the fate of innocent victims; unlike him, we also send in the cavalry. So why begin a War Stories course with a conversation about compassion? At the time, it seemed obvious . . . but then, that's how ideology works—it makes the national seem natural.

What I didn't do is begin with Peter Maass. Roughly fifty pages into his *Love Thy Neighbor*, the war correspondent offers this commentary:

> Bosnia makes you question basic assumptions about humanity, and one of the questions concerns torture. Why, after all, should there be any limit? [. . .] You can, for example, barge into a house and put a gun to a father's head and tell him that you will pull the trigger unless he rapes his daughter [. . .] The father will refuse and say, I will die before doing that. You shrug your shoulders and reply, Okay, old man, I won't shoot you, but I will shoot your daughter. What does the father do now, dear reader? He pleads, he begs, but then you, the man with the gun, put the gun to the daughter's head, you pull back the hammer, and you shout, Now! Do it! Or I shoot! The father starts weeping, yet slowly he unties his belt, moving like a dazed zombie, he can't believe what he must do. You laugh and say, That's right, old man, pull down those pants, pull up your daughter's dress, *and do it!* (51–52)

The point of this passage is captured by voice: its second-person invocation calls the reader into a perspective he has no business sharing. You invade the house, you brandish the gun, you stage-manage the incest while you gaze on, laughing. Except of course that you don't . . . it's not 1992 and you're not in Bosnia, you're just reading a book. Maass's script demonstrates, in succinct fashion, what right-thinking people tend to resist: that the place of the aggressor has its point of view as well.

We rarely see it so directly. Most often, this perspective veers into other forms of expression, either cheerleading or special pleading. The former is especially nefarious; although powerful states have no real need for special pleading, they do need to cheerlead—they sell aggression by transforming it into its obverse, heroism. The case for special pleading is more interesting, though less common; at the very least, such stories acknowledge that aggression is done by humans, not animals. Aggressors are people too.

Take a closer look, and you'll find that violence of this sort is not merely human, it's social. In the case evoked above, Maass describes a ritualized form of degradation, a ceremony involving the denunciation of shameful behavior in front of witnesses. In other words, the abject humiliation here imposed on father and daughter is intended to brand them both as outcasts. An audience is essential: as the sociologist Keith Doubt observed in explicating this passage, "The denouncer and the denounced do not alone constitute a degradation ceremony [. . .] To induce shame, a denouncer needs to convince the witnesses to view the event in a special way" (39). And what way is that? We—the scene purports to prove—are not members of any species that would submit to such treatment, or that could have such shameful things done to it. These Turks, those hadjis—or kikes, slants, savages, what have you—are not like us, and their shameful behavior proves it. Whatever is done to them, they deserve.

And yet, any right-thinking reader will certainly resist such a reading. Isn't it precisely the reverse, you ask? Doesn't the torturer degrade *himself*, not his victims? don't his actions force right-thinking people to denounce *him*? Well, yes, no doubt he does, and no doubt they must . . . unless, that is, those right-thinking people happen to belong to the circle of soldiers around him, complicit in the spectacle before them. Or the nation that supports them. Although Maass doesn't mention this wider cast of characters explicitly, the scene he stages is inconceivable as the work of a single soldier.

On to more familiar territory. At least since the U.S. war in Vietnam, we tend to think of culture as oppositional and assume that most war movies are denunciations of war. I suspect that we do so in error, that it is actually very difficult to make an antiwar film. The silver screen is likely to make even its most horrific subjects shine. And the job of a counterculture may be tougher than we think.

Toward the end of Michael Herr's *Dispatches*, Tim Page, one of the most storied reporters in Herr's clan, speaks with some authority on this subject. After surviving a land mine that left him with shrapnel in his forehead, Page moved into an apartment near the hospital. As Herr puts it, "He began talking more and more about the war, often coming close to tears when he remembered how happy he and all of us had been there" (248). A letter arrives from a British editor soliciting his memoir, asking for a narrative that " 'would take the glamour out of war' " (248). Page can hardly control himself: " 'Take the glamour out of war! I mean, how the bloody hell can you do *that*? Go and take the glamour out of a Huey, go take the glamour out of a Sheridan [. . .] It's like trying to take the glamour out of sex, trying to take the glamour out of the Rolling Stones' " (248). Herr recalls, "We both shrugged and laughed, and Page looked very thoughtful for a moment. 'The very *idea!*' he said. 'Ohhh, what a laugh! Take the bloody *glamour* out of bloody *war!*' " (249).

If Page thinks an antiwar memoir is a joke, what chance then for an antiwar film? Transferred to the screen, transfigured by Panavision and surround sound, and transmuted away from real bodies and real smells, the glamour of war may well be invincible. As Italian singer-songwriter Francesco De Gregori puts it, "La guerra è bella anche se fa male."[1] I have no illusions about what brings students into my War Stories classroom.

John Wayne's 1968 film *The Green Berets* has been described as the sole Vietnam movie made during the war and as its only pro-war film. Although it is neither, it is nonetheless a classic example of a war movie with the aggressor as hero. The novel by Robin Moore that inspired Wayne's film begins "*The Green Berets* is a book of truth" (1). Few would say the same thing about the movie version, though any claim that an aggressor is heroic must make some claim on history. What motivates The Green Berets is precisely this reversal; it is the film's purpose and its content as well. Aggression is the story it intends to reverse.

The opening scene puts the machinery in motion. A press conference showcasing the Green Berets portrays reporters as left-leaning ideologues, and rather stupid ones at that. At one point, befuddled by a sergeant's description of Russian and Chinese munitions in Vietnam, a housewife in the audience comments, "It's strange that we never read of this in the newspapers." His response gets a big laugh: "That's newspapers, ma'am. You could fill volumes with what you don't read in 'em." The Green Berets script, we are meant to understand, will be filled from the same font. The episode ends with newspaperman George Beckworth (played by David Janssen) deciding to accompany the Special Forces team to Vietnam, where the reporter's re-education—and ours—will continue.

The most important schoolroom is located in a Montagnard village, midway through the film. In a lead-up scene, U.S. soldiers are shown giving medical treatment and candy to a group of children from this Central Highland tribe, including the nine- or ten-year-old granddaughter of the village chief. Colonel Mike Kirby (played by Wayne) recruits the leader and offers the villagers military protection. The reporter spends his time with the granddaughter; he even gives her a medallion that he'd been wearing around his neck. When he asks the medic who translates for him if the girl would like this bauble, the officer replies, "She's a woman, isn't she?"

The next morning the Green Berets advance on the village, planning to escort the Montagnards to the U.S. base camp. When they arrive, they instead find the village in flames. The chieftain has been killed and tied to a post; above him a sign is scrawled with the message "DI [sic] green berets." Wayne cuts the chief down and throws the sign away. Captain Nim (played by George Takei), translating for a group of female village elders, asks him, "Do you want to hear the story, sir?" Wayne grumbles, "I know the story, but go ahead." Colonel Mike may have heard it all before, but his audience has not.

Nim reports that, "Charlie came in the night, to take young men. Most of them listened to the chief and refused to go. They killed the chief and did this [he indicates the ruined village] as a reminder to anyone who resisted them." Janssen asks, "What happened to the little girl?" Words and knowing glances are exchanged between the women, the translator, and Wayne, and finally Nim replies, "Vietcong soldiers took her in the jungle. They didn't bring her back." After a brief search in the bush, the medic finds the girl's body and hands the medallion back to Janssen.

Although we may not have realized it, our celluloid classroom has been teaching us geography. Colonel Kirby elaborates on this lesson, with Beckworth looking off into the distance: "Pretty hard to talk to anyone about this country until they've come over here and seen it. The last village that I visited, they didn't kill the chief. They tied him to a tree, brought his teenage daughters out in front of him, and disemboweled them. Then forty of them abused his wife. And then they took a steel rod, broke every bone in her body. Somewhere during the process she died." At that point, the film returns to the U.S. soldiers, who are tending to the wounded. Told that medical evacuations will be necessary, Kirby barks, "Send for my chopper. I can take three." To Beckworth, he adds, "Coming along?" Since he too now knows the story, the once recalcitrant reporter refuses this offer; he comments simply, "I'm staying." Lines like these make clear the filmmaker's intent; they also suggest that President Johnson made a good call in authorizing military assistance for the production of Wayne's film.

To promote any war effort effectively, it is helpful, as Maass puts it, to "question basic assumptions about humanity." In Wayne's world, as in the Bosnia depicted by Maass, far-off countries are defined as sites of cruelty, rape, and murder, places where the torture of young girls and their fathers is commonplace. At the Montagnard village, our hero and his men arrive too late to put a stop to these atrocities. A direct result of their failure is that the scene succeeds in outlining our wider mission—the protection of a vulnerable, virtual, and innocent people against a beastly foe. It also enlists the media in serving this cause.

Moreover, when Wayne's character notes that it's "pretty hard to talk to anyone about this country," his observation is precise. Civilized people don't talk about such things; in point of fact, they can't even conceive of them. For this reason, scenes of torture, though regrettable, are a necessary demonstration. By equating the enemy with the land, such scenes mark out a territory that we may visit, but where we do not belong. Our side feeds, clothes, and heals the vulnerable; we are the mirror opposite of our ruthless, inhuman foe.

Except, of course, when we're not. Although the news would take time to surface, the year that *The Green Berets* was released was also the year of the My Lai massacre. On that particular day, and on many others, a village was laid to waste by U.S. soldiers, not by the Vietcong. In this notorious case, the slaughter of children would appear not as an emblem of our enemy, or of Vietnam itself—instead it would redefine us. The neatness of this reversal almost makes it seem planned. It wasn't. Wayne's film was shot in 1967, and news of My Lai came out only in 1969. Although cheerleading for the aggressor is what *The Green Berets* is all about, the film was more prescient than Wayne himself was aware. So much the better.

Tim O'Brien was in My Lai roughly a year after the massacre, at a time when the army was still successfully covering up. Although its testimony is indirect, his "How to Tell a True War Story" does offer us a hard look from the only perspective we may rightfully have, that of the aggressor. Two atrocities are depicted in this tale, the first large and abstract: an absurd array of aerial bombing, enough to level a mountainside, is called in to end a hallucination.

The second scene of horror is small, specific, even surgical. If you know this story, you'll remember . . . I refer to the torturous slow slaughter by a GI of a "baby VC water buffalo." Names are important—the animal, which the soldiers come across by chance, is labeled "VC" only once, its initial tag. Substantives are used eight more times: twice the buffalo is referred to as "the animal"; all other instances include the word "baby."

The scene begins with a U.S. soldier stroking the buffalo's nose and offering it C-rations, which the animal refuses. The soldier then, we are told, "stepped back and shot it through the right front knee" (78). The description that follows calls the animal "it" sixteen more times. A Petrarchan nightmare of body parts multiplies as well: fourteen are individualized; only one of these, the eyes, are not a target. By the time he's finished, the shooter is crying. At My Lai, Paul Meadlo, after having machine-gunned civilians standing in a ditch, was doing the same.

As this scene unfolds (after—to be precise—the sixth shot), it is interrupted, only once: "He put the rifle muzzle up against the mouth and shot the mouth away. Nobody said much. The whole platoon stood there watching, feeling all kinds of things, but there wasn't a great deal of pity for the baby water buffalo. Curt Lemon was dead. Rat Kiley [the shooter] had lost his best friend in the world. Later in the week he would write a long personal letter to the guy's sister, who would not write back, but for now it was a question of pain. He shot off the tail." After the shooting stops, we return to the platoon, this circle of witnesses: "For a time no one spoke. We had witnessed something essential, something brand-new and profound, a piece of the world so startling there was not yet a name for it." And then, the text continues, "Somebody kicked the baby buffalo" (79).

At least three things bear mention. First, the "name for it" is obvious, even banal. Atrocity.[2] Second, the choice of an animal scapegoat in this tale is another example of indirect representation—that form of war story which, in the previous chapter, I characterized as potentially true. Here indirection is a precondition for telling the aggressor's story at all: although we don't tend to sympathize with those who, in response to their own emotional distress, torture and kill helpless animals, we don't spit at them either. O'Brien's story allows us to see the shooter as—however flawed—a member of our species, simply because his victim wasn't. On this point even warriors and peaceniks may agree. Third, although one man does the shooting, his emotion, and the action itself, are collective. The sequence ends when two members of the platoon dump the buffalo into the village well.

In this regard, O'Brien's "How to Tell a True War Story" returns us to the Bosnian scene that opened this chapter. Both offer glimpses into the psychology of aggression, and both stage in print fictional evocations of real-world events—they translate this world for readers. In doing so, both also make that reader's position equivocal, or at the very least uncomfortable. In *Dispatches*, Michael Herr comments on the shifting nature of his own perspective: "I stood as close to them as I could without actually being one of them, and then I stood as far back as I could without leaving the planet. Disgust doesn't begin to describe what they made me feel, they threw people out of helicopters, tied people up and put the dogs on them

[. . .] But disgust was only one color in the whole mandala, gentleness and pity were other colors, there wasn't a color left out" (67). When aggression is portrayed as human, a variety of problems surface, and the most troubling regard function. Is the aim of representing aggression simply to understand? Can we understand and not condone? And, if we did understand fully, how would our perspective differ from those we represent?

One of the most sustained and insightful analyses of the Abu Ghraib photos—and one of the most provocative theses regarding their lack of reception by the U.S. public—has been penned by the art historian Stephen Eisenman. His book, *The Abu Ghraib Effect*, traces a specific representation of pathos in Western art from Greco-Roman sculpture to the mass culture and racist subcultures of today. For Eisenman, the Abu Ghraib photographs draw on a common mnemonic heritage which has made the inscription of "passionate suffering" a key foundational discourse in Western art.

As an art historian, a central question for Eisenman is how this obvious connection—to works as central to that tradition as the *Laocoön*, or by artists such as Michelangelo and Raphael—was not immediately obvious to his colleagues, and why they instead insistently turned toward *antiwar* representations by Goya and Picasso (or Ben Shahn and Leon Golub) in their discussion of the torture images. Despite topical resemblances that are at times undeniably striking, the latter group of artists, after all, meant to expose and oppose the horrors they depicted. Instead, the tradition that Eisenman dates from the Pergamon Altar (c. 180–150 BCE) through the Italian masters and beyond *celebrates* the expressive depiction of suffering; its "pathos formula of internalized subordination and eroticized chastisement" functions as "a handmaiden to arrogance, power and violence" (122).[3] It sees, not from the observer's perspective, but from that of the aggressor.

One strength of Eisenman's argument is that it makes sense of the comments of Rush Limbaugh, aired on his radio show in early May, 2004. Limbaugh first apparently claimed that the interrogations were "no different than what happens at the Skull and Bones initiation" and went on to characterize the torturers as "need[ing] to blow off some steam," arguing that "emotional release" is understandable in a situation where they are "being fired at every day." "I'm talking about people having a good time," he added. A few days later, Limbaugh returned to the topic, this time comparing the interrogations to "good old American pornography."[4]

Unlike Bill Maher or Don Imus, Limbaugh did not lose his job for speaking his mind. Yet the key elements of his rant—its eroticization of the images, its identification with the torturers, and its imputation of the victims' willing complicity in their own degradation ("a Skull and Bones initiation"; "good fun," etc.)—are point for point those found by Eisenman in works such as Michelangelo's *Dying Slave* and Raphael's *Battle of Ostia*.

Much of the world outside the United States denounced the Abu Ghraib photos for what they are: a record of beastly, state-sanctioned aggression. For U.S. citizens, however, the victims themselves must have been less important than the faces and uniforms of the aggressors—which posed something of a problem. The evidence those faces and uniforms present is in direct opposition to the way most U.S. war stories are framed. In the place of compassion and liberation, the photos instead revealed sadism and bondage. If the U.S. public was able to see anything clearly, if it really even cared to look, it must have been transfixed by the contradiction between, on the one hand, the clean-cut, smiling faces of the soldiers and, on the other, the cruel and degrading actions that these—our—soldiers performed.[5]

Another quality, one that recurs in many of the photos, probably played an even greater role. In several photos, the U.S. soldiers give a "thumbs-up" gesture; two of these photos show a soldier's smiling face just inches away from that of a dead Iraqi prisoner. The only way to describe such photos is to call them trophy shots.[6] Unlike the rest of the world, we citizens of the United States of America cannot look on from the point of view of a compassionate observer. We are being hailed by our own soldiers; when someone makes a "thumbs-up" sign to you, what you're supposed to do is return it.

However different the reception, the Abu Ghraib photos did cause a media firestorm both in this country and abroad. By the winter of 2005, *Jump Cut*, an online journal that reviews contemporary media, had already dedicated an extensive page of links to published work on Abu Ghraib.[7]

Official investigations of the prison abuse mushroomed as well; some low-ranking soldiers were jailed, some high-ranking officials were promoted. Before 2008, however, the story of the photographers was largely told by others; *Standard Operating Procedure*, both the film by Errol Morris and the book by Philip Gourevitch, gave the soldiers themselves a say in the matter. The effect of these two works, based on more than two hundred hours of interviews, is summarized by their common title; after the book and film, it becomes impossible to see the abuse as merely the work of "bad apples," to see it as anything but government-endorsed policy— "standard operating procedure." The real issue, in other words, is command responsibility: if, as a Human Rights Watch report put it back in 2005, Rumsfeld and company were *Getting Away with Torture?*

The history of prison abuse in Iraq, as well as Guantanamo and Afghanistan, is only now beginning to be written. The point of briefly discussing here the early drafts of that history is twofold. First, the worldwide reaction to the Abu Ghraib photos demonstrates both the policy effects of media images—the so-called CNN effect—as well as the limits of those effects. After all, President Bush was reelected. In the days that followed, he appointed Alberto Gonzales to head the U.S. Justice Department— Gonzales, the author of a White House memo describing the Geneva limitations on the questioning of enemy prisoners as "obsolete." Our national press, after the election, widely speculated that Donald Rumsfeld would be a single-term appointee. He was not, and few would cite the Abu Ghraib scandal as a major factor in his long-awaited departure. Condoleezza Rice replaced Colin Powell as secretary of state. Major General Geoffrey Miller, former head of the prison at Guantanamo Bay, was given command of Abu Ghraib. How could this happen? Perhaps someone somewhere believed they all were doing a heck of a job.

CNN effect aside, a central argument of this book is that any careful study of images like those taken at Abu Ghraib will have effects of its own. As a case in point, I conclude this chapter by examining at some length a war story from another country, and from another moment in history. Citizens of the United States, having in part repeated this history, need to see what we can learn from it. The most important lesson, perhaps, is that we have some very long days ahead.

When an account of his conversations with the reporter Horacio Verbitsky was published in Buenos Aires in March 1995, Lieutenant Commander Adolfo Francisco Scilingo became the first military officer to take personal responsibility for executing prisoners during the so-called dirty war in Argentina. As Verbitsky himself comments, in the English edition of this work, "Scilingo said nothing that was not already known, but the words of an executioner admitting to his crimes in the first person had an extraordinary impact, as if the exhibition of Scilingo's tormented soul were necessary to put an end to the two different versions of Argentine history in circulation, so that the narrative of the victims would cease to be that of pariahs and madmen and become the common sense of society" (142). For those outside of Argentina, a country where opposing narratives had continued its dirty war by other means, Scilingo's confession must be less shocking than his silence. How could he—not to mention the entire military and state apparatus responsible for "disappearing" some thirty thousand Argentine citizens—have successfully denied responsibility or remained entirely silent *for nearly twenty years*? And what, in the end, made Scilingo alone come forward?

On these questions, Verbitsky's account of his interaction with Scilingo is indeed instructive. The interviews demonstrate that the effects of aggression may in some cases last as long, and be graven as deeply, in the mind of the aggressor as in that of his victims. Moreover, both the twenty-year hiatus as well as Scilingo's isolation suggest that what is buried can also stay buried—unless and until external events force it to the surface.

Erna Gorman, a survivor of the Holocaust, took more than thirty-five years to begin to speak of her experiences. For her, the precipitating event was a television interview, in the early 1980s, of a young skinhead. She comments: "He was a young, athletic, good-looking boy and I remember him dressed in a German uniform, standing with a raised arm and saying, 'I'm here to finish Hitler's work.' Another interview featured a young man spouting white supremacist slogans while standing next to a mother holding a child on her lap. But it was the statement 'I'm here to finish Hitler's work' that stuck in my mind and petrified me" (1). Since that day, Gorman has told her story countless times, both to individuals and to groups, and especially to schoolchildren. She also wrote more than fifteen drafts of a memoir, which has recently been published. None of this, she insists, is experienced as cathartic; instead, she tells us that "it is destructive to keep thinking about these events and re-experiencing the emotions that come with the memories" (2). If she hadn't happened to see that young man in Nazi dress-up, she might never have begun telling her story. But now she seems no longer to have the choice—a world she believed buried in the past is again staring her in the face.

For Scilingo, the precipitating events are more difficult to empathize with, or even to fathom, but they were no less effective. In 1994, a political crisis ensued in Argentina when Verbitsky made public the fact that two military men, Juan Carlos Rolón and Antonio Pernías—both scheduled for promotion by President Carlos Menem—had been involved in some particularly notorious crimes during the dirty war. According to Scilingo, however, Rolón was "getting shafted" (6) since everything he and Pernías had done was authorized by the military as a whole. Scilingo comments that if "the whole navy was involved in it, then can some be promoted and others not? Can the Senate promote some and not others? [. . .] Were there one, two, or three men who tortured or killed while the rest didn't?" (33). Verbitsky challenges this statement, asking if he means to say that everyone tortured and killed. Scilingo's response reveals his monolithic sense of the military apparatus: "No. All of us were part of the navy when that was being done, and we were rotated through different tasks. In a war, one guy cleans, another guy cooks, other guys kill. But that doesn't mean that they weren't all in the war [. . .]" (33).

Time and time again, Scilingo claims that judgment must be passed on the entire military, or not at all. As his comments make clear, Scilingo also does not see the military as uniquely culpable:

> The armed forces weren't the only ones responsible. A large part of the country consented to the barbarities that were being committed [. . .] I don't think society acted out of terror. I think that it appealed to the armed forces or that it backed what they did. A certain excessiveness in the procedures, as it was called at the time, was not rejected. It was accepted. Very few voices were raised against it. If the majority of the population had demonstrated against it, things would have been different. (23)

Although citizens in democracies are undeniably responsible for their government, Argentina—under a military regime which had taken power by force—was no democracy. And there were voices raised against it. Pernías, for example, as an intelligence official at ESMA, has admitted using kidnapping, torture, and execution, and agreed that the writer and journalist Rodolfo Walsh—Argentina's Ernest Hemingway—was among those taken to ESMA and killed. He has also been accused of the abduction, torture, and murder of two French nuns, although he continues to deny his participation in these crimes.

Beyond the political and media response to these pending promotions, two additional events opened fissures in Scilingo's monolithic worldview. In 1990, the junta leaders who had been convicted in 1985 were pardoned by the Peronist president Carlos Menem. For Scilingo, the acceptance of these pardons by his commanding officers implied that they also accepted their guilt. In addition, Scilingo had written personally to several of them, requesting the publication of a list of those executed by the regime. To him, it was important to end the official secrecy regarding the methods of "detaining, interrogating, and eliminating the enemy" (154).[8] If these actions hadn't been criminal, now that their side had "triumphed in the dirty war," there was no longer a reason to keep quiet.[9] That his commanders refused to do as he asked, or even to acknowledge his letters, made Scilingo's world for the past twenty years seem hollowed out, false—irreconcilable with daily headlines from the news.

To illustrate the relation between the horrors of Argentine reality and the bright and shining edifice of its then official history, Verbitsky borrows a sketch from Julio Cortázar, published in Madrid in 1981:

> A group of Argentines decides to found a city on a promising stretch of level ground, without realizing that most of the land on which they are starting to build their houses is a cemetery of which no visible trace remains. Only the leaders know this, and they keep quiet about it because the place fits in with their plans, because it is a surface smoothed down by death and silence. So buildings and streets go up and life is organized and prospers [. . .] It is then that the symptoms of a strange unease begin, the fears and suspicions of

> those who feel that strange forces are pursuing them and in some
> way denouncing them and trying to drive them away. (141)

Verbitsky also notes that Cortázar decided not to finish this story because, as the Argentine fabulist put it, "he found out it had already been written in the book of history" (142).

Cortázar writes that "the dead know how to come back, in their own way, and to enter the house, the dreams, the happiness of the city's inhabitants" (Verbitsky 141–42). Yet, as the audience for the Hollywood version of this story will recall, even ghosts need a portal. In Tobe Hooper and Steven Spielberg's *Poltergeist* (1982), malevolent spirits first converse with a young girl through the medium of television; in the case of Adolfo Scilingo, a similar portal was formed literally by accident, during the first of two flights where he performed state-sanctioned murder.

Given the length of his silence and the weight of his confession, it is not surprising that Scilingo gives Verbitsky a fragmented, somewhat confused account of his actions, or that he does so reluctantly. What causes his reluctance is key. As he puts it, "I can't get rid of the image of the naked bodies lined up in the plane's aisle, like something in a movie about Nazis" (49). This was no movie. Before the prisoners were thrown into the sea, they were drugged and stripped of their clothes. Verbitsky repeatedly asks Scilingo if the drugs caused prisoners to lose consciousness entirely, or if they were cognizant of what was being done. Scilingo replies that they "were like zombies," that "No, no, no," "No one was aware he was going to die"; he calls "this line of questioning [. . .] somewhat gruesome, totally gruesome" (25). For Scilingo, Cortázar's "strange forces" are the living dead, zombies, and they do indeed "know how to come back."

And, as I have said, the portal was real. During that first flight, a petty officer, upon realizing what he is expected to do, begins weeping uncontrollably and has to be sent into the cockpit. Scilingo then strips the prisoners and helps to lower them through the rear hatch of the plane. Here are the sentences which follow his comment about "the naked bodies lined up in the plane's aisle":

> It was done from Skyvan planes belonging to the coast guard and
> Electras belonging to the navy. In the Skyvan, it was through the rear

hatch, which slides down to open. It's a big door, but it has no inter-
mediate positions. It's closed or it's open, so it was kept in the open
position. The noncommissioned officer kept his foot on the door, so
that there would be about forty centimeters opening onto empty
space. Then we started to lower the subversives through there. I was
pretty nervous about the situation I was experiencing and I almost
fell out into empty space. (49)

Verbitsky's response to this revelation is a single word—"How?" Scilongo:
"I slipped and they caught me." The next question changes the subject—
effectively leaping over, and keeping open, the abyss—to ask Scilongo for
information about the second flight.

Scilingo's spontaneous account of this moment—an instant where he
nearly shared the fate of his victims—is marked by a visible and eloquent
series of repetitions: door/door, open/open/open/opening, empty space/
empty space. Strikingly, he also summarizes his actions not as active, but
as something that he himself suffered through—he calls it "the situation
I was experiencing." Whether or not the prisoners were aware of their
fate, whether they were in fact "like zombies," Scilingo himself is certainly aware. This moment he shared with them has haunted him ever
since. In a later chapter, Verbitsky narrativizes his interviewee's reaction:

He drank two glasses of whiskey, brim-full, when he came back that
night [. . .] But it didn't numb him enough. Later he gave up alcohol
for psychopharmacological drugs [. . .] As soon as he fell asleep, he
relived the flight. While he was throwing the naked bodies out the
hatch, he missed his step and fell. That day in 1977 a member of the
crew had managed to hold him back. But as soon as he fell asleep,
he was devoured by empty space. Before he reached the ocean's
waters, he would wake up. (127)

To abduct, to torture, or to murder, one must separate oneself from the
object of one's violence. Maass's scene seems a sufficient demonstration
of this point. Yet Scilingo's story suggests that, in some cases at least, we
must also question our basic assumptions about inhumanity.

In a bizarre turn of phrase, Scilingo refers to the navy's policy of rotat-
ing personnel on the execution flights as "a kind of communion." Puzzled,

Verbitsky asks him what this "communion" consisted of. Scilingo replies that "no one liked to do it, it wasn't a pleasant thing. But it was done, and it was understood that this was the best way. It wasn't discussed. It was something supreme that was done for the sake of the country. A supreme act. It's very difficult to understand and to explain" (23–24). Verbitsky reminds him that the word "communion" generally carries a mystical, charismatic charge. Scilingo comments simply that, "Yes, that's how it was" (24). "The next day," he adds later, "I didn't feel very good and I was talking with the chaplain of the school, who found a Christian explanation for it [. . .] he was telling me that it was a Christian death, because they didn't suffer, because it wasn't traumatic, that they had to be eliminated, that war was war and even the Bible provided for eliminating the weeds from the wheat field" (30). Verbitsky asks if other soldiers were similarly disturbed. Scilingo avers that, "At heart, all of us were disturbed," but he also notes that talking about it was "taboo" (30).

In *Beyond the Pleasure Principle*, as an illustration of the essential dynamic of trauma, Freud borrows from Torquato Tasso's Renaissance epic *Jerusalem Delivered*. In Book Thirteen, its hero Tancred ventures into a dark, enchanted wood and slashes at a tree with his sword. By doing so, he releases a spirit that speaks in the voice of his lover Clorinda, whom he earlier has killed in a duel without knowing her identity. As the tree bleeds, the voice protests against these repeated blows, and the hero yields, vanquished by his own emotion. According to the psychoanalyst Cathy Caruth, "the exemplary scene of trauma *par excellence*" is the accident; it traps and freezes the mind like a spirit bound inside a tree. A second blow is necessary to release the voice. "The wound of the mind," she comments, "is not a simple and healable event [. . .] but an event which is experienced too soon, too unexpectedly [. . .] and is therefore not available to consciousness until it imposes itself again" (4). For Caruth, "[trauma] is always the story of a wound that cries out, that addresses us in the attempt to tell us of a reality or truth that is not otherwise available" (5).

In this psychoanalytic appropriation of Tasso, important aspects of the original story are missed, or go unmentioned. First of all, it is not the case, as Caruth states, that "Tancred does not hear the voice of Clorinda until the second wounding" (4); he has in fact already heard her, several times.

After their duel, but before Tancred knows it's her, Clorinda asks her opponent to give her the last rites; afterward, "through the act of her joyful and living death," she "seem[s] to say: 'Heaven is opening; I depart in peace'" (12:68, 269). Finally, later that night, as Tancred is dreaming, Clorinda comes and speaks to him directly, forgiving him for her death and thanking him for helping her to reach paradise.

Strangely, both Freud and Caruth take as true—as the real voice of Clorinda—an apparition that in the original story is explicitly false. In describing the voice that emanates from the tree, Tasso himself is careful to note that, despite its power, this "simulacrum is no true shape" (13:44, 290); he also calls it a "false shape and insubstantial plaint" (13:46, 290). Caruth reads this scene as an illustration that "trauma may lead [. . .] to the encounter with another, through the very possibility and surprise of listening to another's wound" (8). *Does it not matter at all that this voice is not Clorinda?*

We might also note that Tancred is a knight in the Crusades, and thus an agent of imperial conquest: he is a killer, not a victim. So let's be clear. On a certain level, it must appear outrageous, even obscene, to describe any mass murderer as traumatized. No less obscene are Scilingo's claims that the execution flights were a form of "communion" (rather than a crime against humanity) or that, "at heart," the executioners were all disturbed by their actions. Yet it is undeniable that Scilingo's story fits like a glove the Freudian narrative of trauma. An accidental slip opened the door, and he imagines himself sharing the fate of his victims. Certainly the communal fellowship of executioners which he envisions, just as much as the ostensibly painless and ostensibly Christian death of his victims, are blatant attempts to erase the real violence of his actions. Similarly, Clorinda's deathbed conversion (her "salvation") reverses the real effect of Tancred's heroic deeds—she, like Jerusalem itself, will be "liberated" by deadly conquest. Yet perhaps in this case, as Freud and Caruth (and Baudrillard) would have it, the simulacrum *is* the truth. Unlike Clorinda herself, the spirit that emanates from the bleeding tree sounds *a voice of protest*—and what it calls for is an end to the bloodshed. This is what stops Tancred in his tracks.

On some level, it is impossible for civilized people to read accounts of torture and murder and imagine someone *not* disturbed by such acts, yet it must be true that many torturers grow to love the power they wield, and that others simply become hardened. After all, there have not been thousands who confessed in Argentina. The first to do so was also the first to be imprisoned under international law for crimes against humanity. In 1997, when Lieutenant Commander Adolfo Scilingo traveled to Spain to testify, he was arrested and subsequently remanded for trial. In 2005, he became the first person ever to be convicted under Spain's law of universal jurisdiction.

An additional crime, one too rarely thought of, must be laid at the door of any regime that authorizes torture and murder. Besides their victims, such regimes also produce perpetrators, and these lives also are lost—yet another sort of crime against humanity.

Conclusion
Bringing the Stories Home

The end of history [. . .] has been for the last half-century a technical possibility. The potential self-destruction of the human kind, in itself a turning point in history, has affected and will affect the life and the fragmented memories, respectively, of all future and past generations—including those "that are past ten thousand years backwards or forwards," as Aristotle wrote [. . .] But to express compassion for those distant fellow humans would be, I suspect, an act of mere rhetoric. Our power to pollute and destroy the present, the past, and the future is incomparably greater than our feeble moral imagination.

Carlo Ginzburg

I deeply respect American sentimentality, the way one respects a wounded hippo. You must keep an eye on it, for you know it is deadly.

Teju Cole

In the final seconds of Kony 2012, the son of the video's director says, "I'm going to be like you, Dad. I'm going to come with you to Africa." The screen is filled by the image of a total eclipse, the sun just beginning to reappear. Director Jason Russell's voice-over then intones, "The better world we want is coming. It's just waiting for us to stop at nothing." Viewers are then instructed to do three things: (1) sign a pledge; (2) get an "action kit"; and (3) donate money to the film's advocacy group. And— oh yes, they should also share the video.

Isolating this moment—the climax of Kony 2012, along with the cosmic hook that leads to its final pitch—seems a bit unfair, but it does demonstrate one thing: the film could really be selling practically anything. A "better world" is possible, so long as we "stop at nothing." And a son who tells his father what every father wants to hear: an affirmation of the father's own choices, a certain form of immortality. "Africa," of course, is the odd note here, particularly if you really haven't seen the rest of the video. And, despite the film's stated goal (to "make Kony famous"), there are still a few people who haven't.

Kony 2012 was posted on YouTube and Vimeo on March 5, 2012, by an NGO called Invisible Children. Since 2004, the group had been working to make a U.S. public aware of the horrific war crimes perpetrated by the Lord's Resistance Army (LRA) and its leader Joseph Kony in Uganda and neighboring countries. But the success of Kony 2012 was a quantum leap, unprecedented in any sort of social networking; it achieved a level of recognition previously inconceivable within the world of human rights organizations. Within weeks the film had been viewed over 100 million times, making it to date the single most viral video in history. I begin my concluding chapter by recapitulating this phenomenon for a very simple reason: Kony 2012 is also a film that Rousseau would have loved, and that Mandeville would have loved to hate. In making this video for the Facebook age, Jason Russell and Invisible Children have given incontrovertible proof that sentimentalism, in war stories at least, is as wildly popular today as it was in the eighteenth century.

A brief description of the characters that populate Kony 2012 will sound, quite frankly, like a recapitulation of the rest of this book. The film's titular subject is the beastly war criminal, Joseph Kony, a man who continues to maim and kill, and who also abducts children, forcing them to become soldiers and sex slaves. ("Making Kony famous," Invisible Children believes, will also make him a marked man, and facilitate his capture.) The film also briefly introduces a young African boy named Jacob, whose brother has been killed by the LRA, and who is himself in danger of being abducted and victimized by them. And then there is the heroic filmmaker, Jason Russell, who witnesses the boy Jacob's suffering and responds by promising that "we will stop them." But the film's real protagonist—the face with far more screen time that any other—is Russell's son Gavin, a representative of vulnerable children everywhere, but principally a stand-in for the film's audience. If Gavin gets the message, we certainly should.

The critical uproar against Jason Russell and his film arose quickly, and showed nearly as much creativity and fervor as the video itself. Within a few days a nineteen-year-old student had posted a Tumblr critique of the film, titled "Visible Children"; his site quickly received over a million visits. Around the same time, Ethan Zuckerman also composed a thoughtful, even-handed blog post critiquing the film, ending with this call to both thought and action:

> the Invisible Children story presents a difficult paradox. If we want people to pay attention to the issues we care about, do we need to oversimplify them? And if we do, do our simplistic framings do more unintentional harm than intentional good? Or is the wave of pushback against this campaign from Invisible Children evidence that we're learning to read and write complex narratives online [. . .] Will Invisible Children's campaign continue unchanged, or will it engage with critics and design a more complex and nuanced response?

In the days to come, a wickedly funny drinking game for Kony 2012 would be posted online as well, lampooning the film's stereotypes, simplifications, and self-aggrandizement. The Nigerian American novelist Teju Cole used Twitter to offer seven pithy comments on the film and what he called the "White Savior Industrial Complex" (the seventh is quoted as an epigraph to this chapter). A chorus of critique from regionally based activists and NGOs arose as well, decrying the lack of African agency in the film as well as its Kiplingesque overtones. More than one also saw ominous implications in Invisible Children's endorsement of American military aid to the Ugandan government as the solution to the Kony/LRA problem. In Uganda itself, a screening of Kony 2012 reportedly met with anger and rock-throwing, forcing the audience to flee the scene.

Not surprisingly, there was also a pushback against the backlash. Both the New York Times columnist Nicholas D. Kristof and Human Rights Watch came out in defense of the aims, if not the methods, of Invisible Children and Kony 2012. Those who have for many years worked to lobby powerful nations and their citizens in hopes of aiding (not saving) the less powerful understandably refused to believe that nothing good could come from all this attention and enthusiasm. In response to critics like Tejo, Kristof commented,

> When a warlord continues to kill and torture across a swath of Congo and Central African Republic, that's not a white man's burden. It's a human burden. To me, it feels repugnant to suggest that compassion should stop at a national boundary or color line. A common humanity binds us all, whatever the color of our skin—or passport.

On March 15, the story was complicated further: Russell was taken to a San Diego hospital, after suffering a very public breakdown. A statement by Ben Keesey, CEO of Invisible Children, attributed the episode to Russell's exhaustion, dehydration, and malnutrition. On April 5, Invisible Children released a second video, *Kony 2012: Part II—Beyond Famous*. Its narrative responds carefully to each of the criticisms outlined above. (Russell and son are absent from the sequel, which focuses largely on the African staff and supporters of Invisible Children's efforts.) Nonetheless, the group's attempt to stage a massive, global awareness event on April 20—where "Kony 2012" posters and messages would blanket the planet—was underwhelming, to say the least.

So what to make of all this? First, readers of this book should be less surprised than most at the unprecedented response to Jason Russell's film. From Jean-Jacques Rousseau in the eighteenth century to Joshua Greene in the twenty-first, a strong argument has been made for the power of sentimental storytelling; both Rousseau and Greene suggest such power is not only innate, it is evolutionarily older than we are. One of the most insistent claims of *Kony 2012*—that human societies are today more closely connected than ever before—is surely incontrovertible, even if increased globalization seems to come hand-in-hand with new (and in some ways more violent) forms of social fragmentation.

But the real lesson here is found in the instantaneous reaction against *Kony 2012*, by those who felt excluded and misrepresented by the film, and that this wave of protest was then followed by another. When a twenty-first-century war story tries to dress up in eighteenth-century garb, perhaps we won't have to wait long before someone pulls the mask off. In this chapter, I conclude by examining a few cases that teach us to read, and perhaps to write, more complex narratives—stories that understand their place in history.

Instantaneous unmaskings are certainly good news. But sometimes, even when the news is good, we need to start looking deeper. For example, despite the generalized euphoria surrounding the Obama inaugural celebrations, some headlines were dark and troubling, at least for observers with a sense of U.S. military history. On January 23, 2009, the new president authorized a bombing strike by an unmanned drone in Pakistan. That same day the *New York Times* reported that "American officials believe that the drone strikes have killed a number of suspected militants along the frontier since last year, including a senior Qaeda operative who was killed Jan. 1 [. . .] But the civilian toll has angered Pakistanis. A senior Pakistani official estimated that the attacks might have killed as many as 100 civilians; it was not possible to verify the estimate."[1]

The following week, this attack served to focus the forum on Bill *Moyers Journal*, a PBS news analysis and interview show. Moyers began his program by remembering 1964, when he served as President Johnson's press secretary; he recalled specifically the decision to bomb North Vietnam after the encounter in the Gulf of Tonkin. As the host commented, "LBJ said we want no wider war, but wider war is what we got, eleven years of it." In the ensuing discussion, Marilyn Young, a historian of the Vietnam war, emphasized what she referred to as "the material meaning" of bombing raids. What went missing in the news reports, she noted, was "what it feels like to be bombed, [. . .] to be on the ground looking up. And the footage that we have [. . .] is of someone 10,000 miles away pushing a button and, wham, there it goes. But nobody's sitting there on the ground looking at what happens." Pierre Sprey, a former Pentagon official who helped design the F-16 Fighter and the A-10 Tankbuster, commented, "And what happens on the ground is for every one of those impacts you get five or ten times as many recruits for the Taliban as you've eliminated. The people that we're trying to convince to become adherents to our cause have turned rigidly hostile to our cause."[2]

More than four years later, it is still too soon to tell how far the Obama administration will go in repeating the mistakes of the Johnson years—yet drone warfare has certainly become a preferred option for the White House today. It also seems clear that essential themes of this book—the limitations on knowledge caused by perspective and narrative positioning—will continue to haunt our representations of war.

There can be few people who know this better than Marc Garlasco. During the initial phase of the war on Iraq, he led the Pentagon team that selected bombing targets; two days after Baghdad fell, however, he left the military and became senior military analyst for Human Rights Watch. With his new job, he traveled to Iraq for the first time to assess the military effectiveness and human cost of the bombing. As he himself tells this remarkable story, Garlasco emphasizes the physicality of his two diametrically opposed perspectives. To Terry Gross, host of NPR's *Fresh Air*, he commented,

> I got on a plane, and next thing I know I'm, you know, with a group of folks I'd never met before, and there's an Iranian and a Belgian and a Russian and a French guy and I'm working with an African American former naval officer and a redhead, and we're going through Iraq. And I'm like, "Oh, my God. Here I am. I'm walking through the streets that I, you know, watched for all these years from above." And all of a sudden I'm walking in the craters that I helped to plan and helped create.[3]

Like Marilyn Young, Garlasco juxtaposes the view from above with on-the-ground reality; he first describes "going through Iraq," then "walking through the streets," and finally "walking in the craters." Yet his most dramatic anecdote comes when Gross asks him to describe a target choice "that didn't go so well." Garlasco recalls an attempt to kill Ali Hassan al-Majid, Saddam's cousin, so-called Chemical Ali:

> We put the target package together, and I was actually sitting in the Pentagon with my targeting cell, and we ended up watching it on the computer screen. We had Predator feeds overhead. And, you know, there were two five-hundred-pound bombs that went down on it. First one went down about three blocks away, and oh, we were so angry. You know, how does a laser-guided bomb fall three blocks

away? And we were very frustrated with that. But moments later, the second weapon came in; and I'll never forget, I was watching this guy, he was walking outside the building, and we were saying, "Buddy, you are in the wrong place at the wrong time." And moments later, pft, just white. The whole screen goes white because we're watching it in infrared. And so everything that's hot is white, and everything that's dark [sic] is black. And for a moment, the sensors on the Predator were basically overwhelmed with the information, and everything's white.

And suddenly you can see the picture start to coalesce, there's this huge explosion of fire, and we can see this rag doll, this dark rag doll person just coming down to earth. The legs—I'll never forget— were just flailing in the air, and came down and hit on the ground and bounced. And, you know, I'll be honest with you, we thought we had killed Chemical Ali. And we cheered and patted ourselves on the back, and we even bet breakfast on how many times that person ended up bouncing.

Although dramatic in the telling, this scene can hardly be unique. The United States alone now musters many thousands of unmanned drone planes; sport fan–style celebrations by what P. W. Singer terms "cubicle warriors" are likely to be increasing every hour.

Less common, perhaps, is a story where a first-person plural viewer— the "we" that watches, then gets frustrated, and ultimately cheers, patting itself on the back—is repeatedly interrupted by a first-person singular fascination with a civilian victim. Garlasco twice comments "I'll never forget," both times in direct reference to the Iraqi man he saw on his screen. Gross asks him if he ever found out who the man was, and Garlasco replies, "No, but I have absolute and total belief that he was a civilian. I mean, I have no reason to believe it was otherwise." His next comment is more personal: "I mean, standing in that crater, there was this little bunny, and it was gray, gray with all of the debris and soot; and it just really hit me because I have these two little girls and, you know, everyone's got a floppy bunny in bed. And it just, it really struck me. It was very difficult at that time." "Everyone's got a floppy bunny" . . . but not everyone orders bombs to be dropped. What Garlasco was struck by—"standing in that crater"—is that in some sense he now occupies both positions at once.

During a later *Fresh Air* interview with P. W. Singer, Terry Gross replays part of the tape from her interview with Garlasco. Singer, author of a book on the robotics revolution in warfare, notes that Garlasco is hardly alone in being able to watch airstrikes from afar. He comments that

> the Iraq War, because of all these systems, is the first one where you can watch but you don't have to be there. And these machines see all. And we're taking these clips and watching from afar, but we're also emailing them around.
>
> We found over 7,000 different clips of combat footage in Iraq, and the soldiers actually call them war porn. And the worry of it is that it connects people to war. They get to see what's happening, but it actually widens the gaps, that is, it creates a further distance. They watch more but they experience less.[4]

People watching more, more and more often, and yet experiencing less . . . yep, sounds like porn to me.

In at least one instance, the relation between war porn and actual porn was commercial. In 2003, a twenty-seven-year-old Floridian named Chris Wilson opened *nowthatsfuckedup.com*, a website dedicated to amateur pornography where users could gain access to several levels of explicit content either by paying or by sending in their own photos and videos. At some point in 2004, Wilson decided to grant U.S. soldiers free access to the site, provided that they sent in photographic evidence that they were actually U.S. soldiers. What followed? Postings of the charred remnants of Iraqis, or of mutilated heads, torsos, or severed limbs, accompanied by cold jokes from photographers and viewers alike.[5] In February 2005, the Pentagon attempted to block soldiers from accessing the site, and it was closed down in April 2006. The webmaster himself was briefly jailed, although the three-hundred-odd charges against him related exclusively to sexual imagery and did not mention the war carnage. In his book investigating this short-lived episode in Iraq War self-portraiture, Gianluigi Ricuperati claims that Chris Wilson was the only person ever sent to jail—in either the United States or Europe—for a pornographic website not involving minors or other clear illegalities (30). Pressure from the Defense Department, the Italian journalist intimates, may have had a hand in such an unprecedented prosecution.

For Ricuperati, although disturbing and distasteful, *nowthatsfuckedup.com* possesses documentary value; he sees the website as delivering, in general, "what really happens when we write that word 'war,'" and, in particular, "what really happens when we write that other word, 'Iraq'" (29–30). As for Chris Wilson, Ricuperati calls him "one of the next century's most paradoxical and viscous characters: the man who bought the truth about war by selling the truth about screwing" (30). The soldiers— and other members of this online community—he describes as hunters: "[These soldiers] go hunting in the various senses which give hunting its grammar, and they offer to the public of their virtual community the best trophies—the rarest, the hardest to pass over"; extraordinary situations, "those that tell a story," are the gold standard for this virtual community (22). Insofar as Ricuperati accurately describes the case, the name for Wilson's website seems to have been prophetic. In the phrase's literal meaning, "Now *that's* fucked up" registers a viewer's sense that something is badly broken; as a moral judgment, the idiom suggests the world shouldn't contain such sights at all. In short, if these are documents, then they are documents of exception—violation, of a convulsive redefinition of both self and world. We're not in Kansas anymore.

Nor are we in the eighteenth century. In the era of Richardson and Rousseau, the language of sensibility and sentimentalism performed its own recategorization of the social order. Our question today is that of Chernyshevsky, Tolstoy, and Lenin: given the world as it now is, what is to be done? Redefining the language for representing war is only a small part of this answer, but it is a necessary part. Where then, as we survey the field, do we find models, stories that do not fall into the trap of giving easy, outdated, and sentimental definitions of their subject? Each of the last three chapters has offered examples. With a focus respectively on victims, then viewers, and finally aggressors, this book has both examined eighteenth-century constraints on the stories we tell and also outlined various ways in which recent accounts have begun to move past them. This final chapter focuses on authors who are engaged directly in changing these stories, and who thus offer something of a model for war representation in the present century.

To my mind, over the course of an entire career no writer has focused more consistently on such questions than J. M. Coetzee, winner of the 2003 Nobel Prize for Literature. In chapter 1, I cited an op-ed from one of the author's protagonists, a fictional response to an actual *New Yorker* article discussing the U.S. government's sanctioning of torture. According to Coetzee's character, "the issue for individual Americans" had become "how, in the face of this shame to which I am subjected, do I behave? How do I save my honour?" A novel Coetzee wrote in 1980 already addressed these questions; in some sense, *Waiting for the Barbarians* was the author's response to the very queries one of his own characters would pose a quarter century later.

Set in the unspecified frontier settlement of an unnamed empire, the story is told in the first person by the town's magistrate—this character is also unnamed. The narrative begins with the arrival of Colonel Joll, an officer from the Third Bureau of the Civil Guard; the magistrate must reconcile himself to a form of governing not entirely his own. Accompanying Joll are two prisoners, an old man and a boy. Officials of the Third Bureau, the magistrate tells us, are "guardians of the State, specialists in the obscurer motions of sedition, devotees of truth, doctors of interrogation" (9). We also learn that the capital fears a united attack from barbarian tribes on its north and west. During questioning, the boy is cut repeatedly with a small knife until he confirms he has knowledge of this attack, and the old man is killed. The magistrate does not himself participate in the interrogations; he leaves this night work to the Colonel, and begins to investigate only after the fact. As he puts it,

> If I had gone on a hunting trip for a few days, as I should have done,
> a visit up-river perhaps, and come back, and without reading it, or
> after skimming it over with an incurious eye, put my seal upon [the
> Colonel's] report, with no question about what the word *investiga-*
> *tions* meant, what lay beneath it like a banshee beneath a stone—if I
> had done the wise thing, then perhaps I might now be able to return
> to my hunting and hawking and placid concupiscence while waiting

for the provocations to cease and the tremors along the frontier to
subside. But alas, I did not ride away: for a while I stopped my ears
to the noises coming from the hut by the granary where the tools are
kept, then in the night I took a lantern and went to see for myself. (9)

The narrative that follows is an account of what the magistrate sees, and
of how he acts in response to these crimes. As he himself remarks, "There
was no way, once I had picked up the lantern, for me to put it down again"
(21). Above all else, Coetzee's novel is meant to be read as a search for
knowledge, for truth.

That said, it is also clear that the magistrate has a competitor in this
search. That "devotee of truth" and "doctor of interrogation," Colonel
Joll, gives us his own understanding of the subject in the book's very first
pages. Strictly defined, torture is not merely the intentional infliction of
pain; it is a juridical procedure, as old as the State itself, one where pain is
used as an instrument to illicit confessions. According to Joll, "A certain
tone enters the voice of a man who is telling the truth." He goes on to
clarify his meaning: "I am speaking of a situation in which I am probing
for the truth, in which I have to exert pressure to find it. First I get lies, you
see—this is what happens—first lies, then pressure, then more lies, then
more pressure, then the break, then more pressure, then the truth. That is
how you get the truth" (5). The magistrate comments, "Pain is truth; all
else is subject to doubt. That is what I bear away from my conversation
with Colonel Joll" (5). Although the magistrate is not among them, Joll is
not without his supporters; a pre–Abu Ghraib survey by the Pew Center
found that 63 percent of U.S. citizens believe that torture is sometimes
justifiable.

So, on the one hand, torture. The nature of the other hand is less clear.
At various times, the magistrate refers to his text as potentially a plea, as
a testament, memoir, confession, history, and as a memorial. The narrative also twice recounts the magistrate's failures to write such an account,
so the status of the very text we're reading is anything but clear. One-
third of the book recounts the protagonist's relationship with yet another
victim of torture, a young woman who has had both of her ankles broken
and has been partially blinded. The magistrate keeps this woman in his
home, and his bed for a time, then decides to return her to the nomadic

tribes. When he returns from this journey, war on the barbarians has been declared, and the magistrate himself is imprisoned as a traitor to the Empire.

One day, during the period when the magistrate is living with the barbarian girl, he goes out at dawn to hunt for antelope. He immediately chances upon a waterbuck, at less than thirty paces, and raises his gun. The ram turns and sees him. As the magistrate tells it, what happens next is unprecedented:

> His hooves touch ice with a click, his jaw stops in mid-motion, we gaze at each other.
>
> My pulse does not quicken: evidently it is not important to me that the ram die.
>
> He chews again, a single scythe of the jaws, and stops. In the clear silence of the morning I find an obscure sentiment lurking at the edge of my consciousness. With the buck before me suspended in immobility, there seems to be time for all things, time even to turn my gaze inward and see what it is that has robbed the hunt of its savour: the sense that this has become no longer a morning's hunting but an occasion on which either the proud ram bleeds to death on the ice or the old hunter misses his aim; that for the duration of this frozen moment the stars are locked in a configuration in which events are not themselves but stand for other things. (39–40)

In *Humanity*, Jonathan Glover relates how George Orwell, in his account of fighting in the Spanish Civil War, recalls that one day an enemy soldier came into view, barely able to keep his pants up as he ran. Orwell comments:

> I refrained from shooting at him . . . I did not shoot partly because of that detail about the trousers. I had come here to shoot at "Fascists"; but a man who is holding up his trousers isn't a "Fascist," he is visibly a fellow creature, similar to yourself, and you don't feel like shooting at him. (53)

Both anecdotes make clear the difficulty of saying precisely what will turn a man away from hunting. For Orwell, it was a connection to the panicked, comic nakedness of his prey; for the magistrate, it is a frozen moment that transforms the hunt into sentimental literature.

When the magistrate, still out of sorts from his failed excursion, tells the girl of his encounter with the buck, he fails to make her see its larger sense. She tells him that he shouldn't hunt if he doesn't enjoy it. He comments, "That is not the meaning of the story, but what is the use of arguing? I am like an incompetent schoolmaster, fishing about with my maieutic forceps when I ought to be filling her with the truth" (41). Though his phrasing has a metaphor too many, it does prove prescient. Without warning the girl at last reveals to him what the magistrate has repeatedly asked her to tell: the details of her interrogation. They heated a two-pronged fork and used it to burn a hole in her retinas. Fishing about with a forceps indeed.

Later in the novel, when the magistrate is imprisoned in the same room where the girl and her father were tortured, he attempts to conjure up for himself "the ghosts trapped between these walls" (80).

> Somewhere, always, a child is being beaten. I think of one who despite her age was still a child; who was brought in here and hurt before her father's eyes; who watched him being humiliated before her, and saw that he knew what she saw [. . .]
>
> After that she had no father. Her father had annihilated himself, he was a dead man. It must have been at this point, when she closed herself off to him, that he threw himself upon his interrogators, if there is any truth in their story, and clawed at them like a wild animal until he was clubbed down. (80)

The lines which follow indicate that, on one level, the magistrate's account must be read as a form of special pleading.

> I gave the girl my protection, offering in my equivocal way to be her father. But I came too late, after she had ceased to believe in fathers. I wanted to do what was right, I wanted to make reparation: I will not deny this decent impulse, however mixed with more questionable motives: there must always be a place for penance and reparation. (80–81)

One thing is clear: the magistrate's narrative position is no easier to sort out than the generic categorization of his tale. First and foremost an observer, as a state official he is an aggressor, yet the magistrate is hero of his story as well.

There is in the novel an occasion for heroism in the classic sense. Having secretly obtained a key to his cell, the magistrate blends into a crowd amassed to observe the public beating and humiliation of captured barbarians; naked and prostrate, the prisoners are bound together with a loop of wire through their hands and cheeks. After the soldiers tire, a young girl is encouraged by the crowd to use a stave on them, and then there is "a general scramble for the canes, the soldiers can barely keep order" (106). When Colonel Joll finally faces the crowd, brandishing a four-pound hammer, the magistrate at last protests:

> "No!" I hear the first word from my throat, rusty, not loud enough.
> Then again: "No!" This time the world rings like a bell from my chest
> [. . .] When I turn to Colonel Joll he is standing not five paces from
> me, his arms folded. I point a finger at him. "You!" I shout. Let it all
> be said. Let him be the one on whom the anger breaks. "You are
> depraving these people!" (106)

This moment of heroism does not last. The magistrate is himself beaten, his hand, nose and perhaps his cheekbone broken, before he can do much more than indicate the prisoners and claim them as men: "You would not use a hammer on a beast, not on a beast!" (107). Despite his abject state, he sees their attack on him as a tactical error; the magistrate questions his own ability as orator, and even doubts his commitment to justice for "these ridiculous barbarian prisoners with their backsides in the air" (108).

A subsequent scene completes his degradation, a transition from hero to victim. The magistrate, after further humiliations in the public square, is ultimately taken out of his cell and given a woman's smock to cover his nakedness. With a child's help, a noose is thrown over the branch of a mulberry tree. The prisoner is hooded, taken up a ladder, the rope slowly tightens until he falls and is hung by the neck; he swings in the air, and is slowly lowered to the ground. With arms bound behind his back, the rope is next tied to his wrists. He is again hoisted into the air. As the muscles in his shoulders tear, the magistrate gives voice to his pain:

> From my throat comes the first mournful dry bellow, like the pour-
> ing of gravel. Two little boys drop out of the tree and, hand in hand,
> not looking back, trot off. I bellow again and again, there is nothing
> I can do to stop it, the noise comes out of a body that knows itself
> damaged perhaps beyond repair and roars its fright [. . .] Someone
> gives me a push and I begin to float back and forth in an arc a foot
> above the ground like a great old moth with its wings pinched
> together, roaring, shouting. "He is calling his barbarian friends,"
> someone observes. "That is barbarian language you hear." There is
> laughter. (121)

Before becoming a victim himself, the magistrate made a remark which is the appropriate response to any identification between pain and truth. Conversing with the blind barbarian girl, urging her to tell the story of her interrogation, he tells her, "Don't make a mystery of it, pain is only pain" (32). Although pain may be truth, it is not a metaphysical, not even a human truth. It is dumb, bellowing, as banal as evil, and certainly not species-specific.

The form of torture endured by the magistrate has a lengthy history in what we traditionally refer to as Western civilization. Let me briefly note two examples. With great economy and discretion, Jean Améry has described the manner by which the Gestapo dislocated both his shoulders. He also noted, however, that the key existential moment for this horrific experience in fact came much earlier. As he put it,

> The first blow brings home to the prisoner that he is helpless, and
> thus it already contains in the bud everything that is to come [. . .]
> They are permitted to punch me in the face, the victim feels in numb
> surprise and concludes in just as numb certainty: they will do with
> me what they want. (27)

Améry used a deceptively simple phrase to describe the transformation we undergo when a regime using torture takes us into its hands. What dies at that moment he called "trust in the world." We lose, he explained, the certainty that by reason of written or unwritten social contracts the other person will spare me—more precisely stated, that he will respect my physical, and with it also my metaphysical, being. The boundaries of my body are also the boundaries of my self. My skin surface shields me against the external world. If I am to have trust, I must feel on it only what I want to feel. (27–28)

In the *New Yorker* in 2005, Jane Mayer recounted the following:

Two years ago, at Abu Ghraib prison, outside Baghdad, an Iraqi prisoner in [C.I.A. officer Mark] Swanner's custody, Manadel al-Jamadi, died during an interrogation. His head had been covered with a plastic bag, and he was shackled in a crucifixion-like pose that inhibited his ability to breathe; according to forensic patholo-gists who have examined the case, he asphyxiated. In a subsequent internal investigation, United States government authorities classi-fied Jamadi's death as a "homicide," meaning that it resulted from unnatural causes. (1)

Mayer also referred to an AP report describing the position which killed Jamadi "as a form of torture known as 'Palestinian hanging,' where a prisoner whose hands are secured behind his back is suspended by his arms" (7)—the same form of torture used, by the Gestapo, to unhinge both of Jean Améry's shoulders.

By the end of *Waiting for the Barbarians*, the war is lost and the soldiers have left, and the magistrate has returned to his position of leadership. The townspeople who have not abandoned their homes wait, terrified, for the arrival of the victors. The magistrate has tried, and failed, to compose a record of his settlement.

It is not easy to see what can be salvaged from a story where the hero moves, with the power of destiny, through each of the traditional posi-tions staged in a sentimental tale; he is both observer and aggressor, then finally victim as well. Certainly the magistrate is not, as Colonel Joll mock-ingly terms him, the One Just Man. His crimes are too great, his motiva-tions too impure, and his actions too feeble; our feelings towards him remain mixed. The lesson could perhaps be, as the magistrate himself tells Joll, that "the crime [. . .] latent in us we must inflict on ourselves"

(146). As a political platform, however, self-flagellation seems likely to remain the discourse of minority parties.

And yet it may be that the magistrate is himself changed by his search for truth, and that he is changed for the better. When the magistrate kneels before the tortured girl, unbinds her wounds, and—in an audacious rehearsal of the biblical story—begins to wash her feet, he initiates a course of penance and reparation which will slowly change his relations with the girl, with his townspeople, and with history itself. Although such actions cannot change the past, they do affect the present and may yet help to shape the future. In one particularly resonant self-characterization, the magistrate comments, "So I continue to swoop and circle around the irreducible figure of the girl, casting one net of meaning after another over her" (81). He cannot see she what she sees, and he surely cannot speak for her (he has, quite literally, never even learned her language). He will never know whether she would identify above her "the protecting wings of a guardian albatross or the black shape of a coward crow" (81). Yet his relentless focus on this young victim and his responsibility for her does yield a man capable of true sacrifice at last. We can only hope that Coetzee himself will continue to swoop and circle for many years to come.

The title of the next book is meant to make you stop and take notice—it's called *Shoot an Iraqi*. The cover photo is black and white: one shoulder and half the chest of a man wearing a black jacket and keffiyeh. His body tilted to the right side of the page, head nearly outside the frame, only a bit of dark hair. Covering the cheek, ear, neck and shoulder is a circular yellow splatter. Similar but smaller blotches of yellow dot the top edge of the cover and its bottom left corner. The book's subtitle is *Art, Life, and Resistance under the Gun*; the authors are Wafaa Bilal and Kari Lydersen.

Coetzee's novel works on and through a multiplicity of distances: the story is distant in time and abstract in place, the protagonist himself makes a difficult journey beyond a frontier settlement to meet directly with so-called barbarians. The story of *Shoot an Iraqi* travels a similarly long distance, but it does so only—to quote Edward Albee—in order to come back a short way correctly. And it's not fiction.

Wafaa Bilal is an Iraqi artist who came to the United States as a refugee after the 1991 Iraq war. Kari Lydersen is a journalist and author who reports for the *Washington Post*. *Shoot an Iraqi* tells Bilal's life story—in the first person—to document a work of performance art staged in the spring of 2007. Its first paragraph offers a concise summary:

> On May 4, 2007, I entered FlatFile Galleries in Chicago for a project called Domestic Tension, a live art installation. For one month I would live in a makeshift room set up in the gallery, going about my daily routine with a robotically controlled paintball gun aimed at me, which people could shoot live and over the internet, 24 hours a day. (1)

When the month ended, more than 65,000 shots had been fired at Bilal by people from 136 countries (2).

The gallery in Chicago was far from the first place Bilal had turned into a makeshift studio and living space for himself and his art. During his childhood years, his family lived in a two-room house, and, as Bilal summarizes, "My dad lived in one room, and the rest of us—up to eight people as the family grew—lived in the other" (7). Yet even in these cramped quarters, he tells us,

> I created a little studio of my own under the stairs that led to the roof, so tiny you couldn't stand up in it, but it was a private little place for me to paint. In the summer it was stifling, so I built a crude homemade air conditioner from an old radiator, an air pump, a fan and a tin can I'd fill with water and ice. I like to think of it as my first foray into technological art. When tensions escalated with my father or the bustle of family life became too much, I would slip away to paint and dream there, in my own little world. (31)

We might find in these words a romantic, nineteenth-century portrait of the artist: painting a dreamworld, as if art were timeless, something that takes shape in the mind, not in history. Bilal, on the contrary, already sees the studio itself as a work of art, where technology is not support or intrusion, but integral to the work. A world of his own is what he produces, a sanctuary, created in direct response to the forces of the world that surrounds him.

You don't have to be a psychoanalyst to understand that in traditional societies a son's politics tend to be formed in relation to his father. Wafaa Bilal's early life, as recounted in *Shoot an Iraqi*, is dominated by this relationship, so much so that, after a single sentence on his family as a whole, seven paragraphs focus exclusively on the father. To explain his dad's leftist politics, Bilal comments: "Foreigners might not know that Iraq used to have a strong Communist Party—it was a highly literate, educated country, and wherever you have education, you usually have communists" (6). When Saddam Hussein took control of Iraq, Bilal's father, who was a teacher, was forced to betray his intellectual convictions—the Ba'ath Party saw communism as a threat to its hold on power.

From that time on, the family served as an outlet for the elder Bilal's rage. Physically violent toward his wife, he also took her jewelry, and later even sold a home that was built for the family, in order to gamble and chase women. In subsequent pages, we learn that Wafaa's parents separated many times, actually divorcing officially and remarrying on three separate occasions. We are also told that the father was institutionalized and then "granted disability leave from his teaching job due to his mental instability" (12). Brief acknowledgment is also given of the fact that "Wafaa" is usually a girl's name. His father initially wanted to have rhyming names for his children, so the first four were named Rajlaa, Alaa, Wafaa, and Safaa (after the couple remarried, three more boys, Haji, Ahmed, and Asraa were added to the clan). Despite such treatment, Wafaa spent his youth in close contact with this problem parent. When the elder Bilal retired from teaching, Wafaa even worked as assistant in his new profession of carpentry. As he puts it, "Though our relationship was extremely tense [. . .], I wanted to learn the trade" (12).

The book recounts only a single physical confrontation between the two; it is also the only direct account of the father's violence:

> When I was 13 years old, I made my stand against him. He was in a particularly foul mood that day, and had been hitting my mother and my sister Rajaa. In the evening as he was sitting in the open-air kitchen eating a kabob, we got into an argument. He slowly finished his kabob, eyeing me like an adversary in a boxing ring. Then, with cold and calculated precision, he threw the plate at me. It hit me

> squarely on the forehead and shattered on the floor. With a throb-
> bing bruise already swelling, I grabbed the ceramic shards and
> charged him. He jumped up, startled, kabob remnants cascading off
> his lap, and ran out onto the street. I chased him to the threshold
> and then locked the door behind him. (23)

In a figurative sense, this door would stay locked for many years to come. After that day, the two largely managed to avoid each other. The father, no longer wanting to risk a physical confrontation, would punish Wafaa by banishing him from the home; the son, "preferr[ing] not to further humiliate or challenge" his father, "would stoically comply" (23).

In the final third of *Shoot an Iraqi*, the reader arrives at what is, before Chicago, the single most inspiring moment of Bilal's autobiography, and dedication to art is again the spur to transformative action.[6] By this time, the artist has made it through both the bombing of his hometown and an equally dangerous period at a makeshift transit camp on the Iraq-Kuwait border. He is with his brother Alaa in Saudi Arabia, trying to survive life in a refugee camp with no visible end or exit. He comments, "Like most peo-ple, I have an innate repulsion to imprisonment, the feeling of being trapped or under someone else's control; a refugee camp combines all these feelings" (114).

The camp was a brutal place, full of personal, religious and tribal feuds, and a near Hobbesian level of anarchy reigned. Bilal recalls that "you could never feel safe—every night there were tents set on fire and people disappeared. The guards would kidnap kids or young men with no family and rape them. [. . .] Several times people from the camp followed the trucks after the guards had kidnapped a man, and they saw the guards hand him over to Iraqi soldiers at the border in exchange for liquor or a little money" (123). He adds, "As single men without families, my brother and I were likely targets. [. . .] At night I'd lie in bed listening to the guards' trucks rumbling by, praying they wouldn't stop at our tent. We'd hear them stop somewhere nearby and then we'd hear a man scream as they beat him. And then silence" (123). Given these hellish conditions, it is hard to imagine how Bilal could ever have endured that five-year limit which, upon arrival, he vowed was the most he would stay. Five years, he said to himself, he "could use [. . .] to mature artistically and intellectually: a sort of self-imposed training camp." After that, he "would do whatever it took to leave. Any option would be open" (114).

With money earned picking up trash and disinfecting toilets, Wafaa bought art supplies and continued to paint. Still, the frequent sandstorms that ripped through the tent city, strong enough to endanger the lives of the elderly and people with asthma, also destroyed his paintings. One day he decided to build himself an adobe hut; he began mixing run-off water from the camp kitchens with clay to make bricks. As he tells it,

> People thought I was crazy. They didn't think the mixture would harden, but it did. And they didn't want to think we would be there much longer—but we were. Every day I'd make a few bricks, and some friends would help, especially if I gave them cigarettes. When I had enough bricks, we started stacking them up into sturdy, stout walls. When they were as tall as a regular room, with blocks cut out for windows and a door, we made a roof from the plastic trash bags I got from my job collecting trash. I laid them out on the sand and fused them together with heat from a candle. I covered the window in clear plastic. "Let the sandstorm come," I said to myself, "This place is sealed!" (132)

When winter came, the same doubters returned to ask Bilal for instructions and "soon people were making bricks all over the camp. The Saudis were amazed at how we turned the camp into a village" (133). Bilal's home became a studio and literary salon, frequented by other artists and intellectuals day and night; together they built an additional wall in order to display their artwork. Such efforts, he comments, "helped us keep our dignity, intellectual spark and humanity while we were treated like animals by the uneducated guards" (133).

Among those who must best understand Bilal's achievement are the artists of the Bosnian collective FAMA. Their 1993 *Survival Guide*, a Michelin-style introduction to Sarajevo under siege, declared:

> The besieged city defends itself by culture and thus survives. Groups and individuals create whatever they used to create before the siege. In impossible circumstances they produce films, write books, publish newspapers, produce radio programs, design postcards, stage

exhibitions, performances, make blueprints for rebuilding the city, found banks, organize fashion shows, shoot photographs, celebrate holidays, put on make-up. Sarajevo is the city of the future and of life in the post-cataclysm. (365)

The two situations are hardly identical: in Saudi Arabia, a tent city for refugees was transformed into a village; in Bosnia, a European capital was used as a shooting gallery. In both places, nonetheless, art became the measure of a tenuous, tenacious humanity.

Humanity is also the title of Jonathan Glover's history of the twentieth century. The theoretical discussion that begins this book is of use here as well. In his opening pages, the historian and ethical philosopher summarizes recent discussions of a problem usually called "the prisoners' dilemma." Here's the set-up. Two partners in crime are interrogated separately. Both are told that if they confess, and their partner does not, they will go free and the other will get twelve years. If neither confesses, each goes to jail for one year, if both do, both get five. Once you think this through, you see that selfishness turns out to be self-defeating; if both prisoners worry only about themselves, they will both confess, and get five years. However, if both trust each other, neither will confess, and the two will go to jail for only a single year.

As Glover emphasizes, the prisoners' dilemma depends entirely on a very precise structure of rewards. Moreover, a series of dilemmas with the same players would likely result in the development of different strategies, and varying the reward system would as well. According to Glover, the lesson of the prisoners' dilemma is that "under some conditions co-operation is more successful than selfishness." He adds, "Those of us who want to see co-operation rather than conflict have a reason to rig the social rewards and penalties so that co-operation becomes a winning strategy" (20). Hard to disagree with that. And yet it still surprises us to see a triumph of social rigging in a besieged city or a camp for refugees.

The second paragraph of Shoot an Iraqi gives a simple, moving summary of the motivations and intentions behind Bilal's gallery exhibition: "I had conceived of the project earlier [in 2007], a product of my grief at the deaths of my brother [Haji] and father in my hometown of Kufa, Iraq (a holy city near Najaf) in 2004, and my intense need to connect my life as an artist in the comfort zone of the United States to the terrors and sorrows of the conflict zone in which my family and so many others were living out their daily lives" (1).

The story of these two deaths is recounted in full only late in the book, sandwiched between its description of the horrors of refugee camp life and the tale of the Saudi camp's transformation into a village. With a space break, and no transition, the new section begins, "Again, my mind turns to Haji" (123).

Having lived in the United States since 1992, Wafaa knew his brother only when Haji was young, and then through family members' stories about him. He describes him as follows:

> [Haji] was tough and fearless, much more so than I or my other brothers were. He walked with a swagger and literally had a gun on his hip at all times. During the embargo my family's neighborhood became very rough; it made the south side of Chicago look like a picnic. Even before the war, you would see people shot and slaughtered there on a regular basis. You had to be tough to survive there, and Haji was one of the toughest. (124)

Having said this, Bilal quickly qualifies his description. His insight here is essential:

> Though I detest machismo and male bravado, I had to admire Haji's toughness. His was not an aggressive, flamboyant show of strength, but an iron fearlessness and refusal to back down. If he believed in something, he would stand up for it no matter what. I feel I have this quality intellectually and artistically, but Haji translated his strength into a physical manifestation and bravery very different from mine[.] (124)

That Wafaa has zero tolerance for male swagger is clear on every page of *Shoot an Iraqi*, no less so than his artistic and intellectual courage. The twin losses of brother and father allowed him to see the violence during his childhood as influenced by cultural strictures that are placed on all Arab men. He comments that "people see Arab culture as a patriarchal system that oppresses women, which it is, but men are also oppressed—they oppress themselves with the rigid expectations and roles they must fill or else be shunned. In this vise-like social grip, my father repressed all his frustrations and shattered dreams and humiliations, ending up with nothing but the cruel and crazy outbursts" (127). After the second death, the gathering of family at his brother's home encouraged him to do what is inevitably a difficult task; he spends time "thinking about [his] father, not in relation to [him]self, but as his own person, as an Iraqi, as a man" (127).

From conversations with his mother and his brother Ahmed, as well as his own telephone calls to Haji, Wafaa became convinced that his brother was close to the insurgency, specifically to the Mahdi Army of Moqtada al-Sadr. One day, as U.S. troops closed in on Kufa, al-Sadr's men came to pressure Haji; they wanted him to help man a checkpoint at the Kufa Bridge—the same bridge that Wafaa had spent hours painting during Operation Desert Storm, and where he witnessed the bloody aftermath of a bombing that destroyed an Iraqi wedding party. Ahmed and his mother try to stop Haji from leaving, but Haji won't let them. When the two stand in the doorway, he tells them, AK-47 in hand, "If you don't move out of my way, I'm going to shoot you" (125). That very night, around 2:00 a.m., he is killed in an explosion.

> Haji's friends said they were all at the checkpoint, and when they saw a U.S. unmanned drone fly over taking pictures, they knew a bomb would be coming. So they ran, except for Haji—he was so defiant. He wanted to show he wasn't afraid of anything. Sure enough an American helicopter flew over and dropped explosives on the checkpoint, blowing everything to pieces. (125)

As described here, I imagine this event falls into the category of what the U.S. military terms "a good kill." According to Bilal, shrapnel from the explosions blew a fist-sized hole directly through Haji's chest.

And their father died two months later. "He dropped from 250 pounds to a skeleton of a man, so light that Ahmed could easily carry him. It was a slow, painful process. As they say in our culture, the grief ate him alive. And his slow wasting away was a daily reminder to my family of my brother's death, so they could never put it behind them" (126). In writing, lack of a transition can be a sign that, for the author, there is no space or difference between two things—the prose equivalent of an arithmetic equation. The next paragraph in *Shoot an Iraqi* is only a single sentence, a jump-cut from his father's grief to his own. He tells us, "I only talked to my father three times after I left Iraq" (126).

When the deaths of two family members come close together, they are experienced as a single uncanny event. Wafaa describes the paintball project as "a product of my grief at the deaths of my brother and father"; this complex drives the work, and the project itself is an act of mourning. Like Orpheus in hell, Bilal uses his art to transmute and transform loss. With his voluntary, month-long descent into the psychical and emotional realities of life under siege, the artist stages an experience that invites in equally enemies, comrades, and those who stand outside, the witnesses. Aggressors, heroes, and observers—the choice is deliberately left open.

It is also true that most of those who came to the paintball project during its thirty-one-day run had little or no knowledge of the biography that the preceding pages summarize. Nor should they, some would say. Critics and artists alike frequently claim that any real work of art must stand on its own; the relative autonomy of art is perceived as its holy spirit, as if the minds of artist and audience alike hold only immaculate conceptions. Bilal puts it somewhat differently: he himself comments that it doesn't matter what you've lived though, only what you've made of it. In effect, the entire book-length narrative of the paintball project is a sustained argument against the cult of art-for-art's-sake. To make that argument, in marked distinction from its presentation here, *Shoot an Iraqi* shuttles back and forth between the artist's life story and a diary-like narrative of his show in Chicago.

In my chapter, by giving you the life first, the goal has been to make it impossible for you to see the paintball project as anything other than the culmination of a life lived around, in, and passing through war. A product of grief, yes, yet *Domestic Tension* was also the instinctual expression of physical, intellectual, and emotional reflexes honed by a single idea—that art is the only truly human response to violence.

In my War Stories class, as we read *Shoot an Iraqi* together, I ask students to apply Glover's idea of social rigging to the Chicago gallery exhibition. Like the prisoners' dilemma, Bilal's performance piece constructs an artificial system, one that seems to encourage some behaviors and discourage others. So if humanity is the goal, do the choices Bilal and his team make in shaping *Domestic Tension* increase or decrease it? As is true of all performance, these choices were only in part made before the work opened; any interactive medium demands constant attention, and flexible responses to ever-changing conditions—an open hand as well as a fixed sense of purpose. The paintball project, which relied on participation from its audience, was a particularly dynamic form of art installation; as a result, it also invited in a host of problems that no design and no designer, however creative, could have predicted.

The space used by the exhibition measured 32' x 15'; it resembled a well-furnished prison cell, or perhaps a college dorm room: bed, desk, computer, lamp, and coffee table. There was also an (unused) exercise bike, several Plexiglas screens or shields, a mock door frame, and, of course, the robotically controlled paintgun at the threshold of Bilal's living space. A small viewing area for visitors and a computer from which they could fire the gun were provided as well. The webcam interface for the project was intentionally left bare: its image was a grainy black and white, streamed without sound. Each day Bilal also recorded video, editing it down and posting it on YouTube. In addition, the website had a chat room where shooters and watchers alike could interact with the artist, and a software program recorded the IP address and geographical location of each computer operating the gun. Bilal spent the entire month in the building, although he did occasionally leave his cell to nap, shower, use the bathroom, get food, and give media interviews. "Aside from those brief respites," he comments, "I spent the majority of my time in the range of the gun as an available target" (2). He "wore a paintball vest and goggles throughout the exhibit, along with [his] trademark keffiyeh" (3).

Within these details of the set-up, Glover's criteria resonate. The low-quality website imaging, Bilal comments, was "an intentional decision to heighten the sense of remoteness and detachment" (3); it also, one suspects, made the shooting easier. The chat room and the YouTube videos, on the other hand, seem to balance or even counteract this distancing effect. The videos were in color, and Wafaa sometimes used the camera to record conversations with his visitors; most often, however, he spoke directly to it—a means of addressing his audience and of recording his

Domestic Tension, wide-angle view of the gallery space.

emotional state and physical condition through the month-long ordeal. The chat room was intended as a space for direct interaction between artist and audience, yet it too could become a battlefield, an arena where words were hurled, not exchanged. Given the video diaries and chatting, the remote-control gun and even remoter image may be seen as something of a trap, or perhaps a gamble—intentionally bringing in the hunters in hopes that they can be turned, like Coetzee's magistrate or Orwell's gun.

On occasion it worked as planned. On Day 15, shots were fired for over four hours straight by someone in Columbus, Ohio. People in the chat room told the shooter to cool it, but he wouldn't reply. He just kept shooting. When Wafaa got his dinner and sat down to eat, the paintballs continued to shatter on the wall behind him and splatter everywhere. Fed up with this behavior at last, he looks into the webcam and protests, " 'Hey Columbus, I am having my dinner and your paintballs are falling into it.' " At last a response. "[The shooter] types back, 'Ouch, sorry about that,' and he stops shooting. He tells me that his name is Luke" (78). Bilal comments, "I feel like my interaction with Luke is a real victory" (78).

Minutes later, however, all hell breaks loose. Hackers have managed to turn the single-shot paintball gun into an automatically firing machine gun. At the same time, chat room comments start flying with equal speed. Bilal describes their tone and intent: "They are no longer philosophical, analytical and flirtatious like before; they are increasingly aggressive, obnoxious and sexual. [. . .] I wanted to use the internet to reach people outside the gallery and established art worlds, and I wanted to democratize the process of viewing and interacting with my work. But I didn't know how brutal the anonymous internet culture could be" (78).

What has happened is Digg.com, a website that ranks stories published on the Internet. A *Chicago Tribune* article from the previous day has put the paintball project on this site's front page. Although Bilal has a tech-savvy helper, Jason (an early viewer of the project who became a valued member of the team), it does no good to ban the hacker. The code is then posted for anyone to use; when consecutive multiple shots are banned, the hackers begin using botnets, a network of computers that allows them to shoot automatically from a variety of locations. Jason stays up most of the night to ban the bots, but the words keep coming, and the sound of the shots, hour after hour, is maddening.

> Shoot him again for Jesus.
> Send him to guantanamo.
> Stone this infidel.
> Ohshit its that guy that's on the run with bin laden.
> Can you jump around a little?
> Lyndie [sic] England where are you?
> I'm touching myself.
> It's a trap! Mossad put bullets in your gun.
> I'm going jihad on your ass. (80)

Wafaa:

> They want to kill me. I feel a weight on my chest as if someone's sitting on it. I can't breathe [. . .] I'm losing it. Every sound and every small movement of the gun feels like an attack on my already taut nerves. I have to get away.
>
> "I'm going to get a glass of wine and lay down", I tell the camera in a shaky voice. (80–81)

What was intended as democratization has become mob rule, and, on this day, there will be no heroic magistrate to stand up against depravity.

Except that Bilal himself doesn't stay down for long. Obsessing over the irrationality and ignorance of this flood of anonymous hatred, he decides to take control of the situation with a bit of street theater. First he disconnects the compressed-air canister to stop the paintballs from shooting out. The gun continues to move, and the trigger continues to fire; with yellow paint covering everything, it seems impossible that the shooters would notice. The act goes on:

> I move around the room, pretending to be dodging and ducking and flinching in fear as the gun keeps popping. I speak into the video camera for tomorrow's YouTube clip. "Digg.com, this is very disturbing, very disturbing," I say. I ramble for a few minutes, my eyes darting right and left. "Very disturbing, Digg.com, this is very disturbing." I'm sure I am giving an Oscar-worthy performance and that once I post it on YouTube, it will change their minds to see the level of terror on my face. (81)

Months later, the artist would watch this video again. In the moment, he notes, he believed that he was in control; later he has trouble even watching the manic, strung-out man on the screen—"spouting one fevered monologue after another, eyes glazed and constantly staring at the ominous clicking gun" (85).

And it doesn't end there. Wafaa next engages a shooter who accuses him of fraud. Apparently, this guy Eric has tried to fire at a white spot on the wall, and saw no result. In this moment of weakness, Bilal starts a macho pissing contest: "I challenge him to visit me, to spend a day with me in this room. I tell him that someone like him has never been in a situation like this before. He claims he has. From San Diego, maybe he's in the military" (82). Even after a phone call, this exchange goes nowhere, and Wafaa isn't the kind to put up with this for long. He tries again to shut them out, to read a little, have a glass of wine.

Which doesn't work either. Unable to find peace, unable to relax, he eventually returns to his art:

> Click click click . . . They want to see me suffer, so I decide to give

them what they want. But on my terms—I'm not their clown. I'll act
the part of the "stupid Iraqi" so they will think that they've won, that
they've defeated me [. . .]

I step in front of the camera and tumble to the ground, face
down. I want them to think I've been hit. I was a soccer player, so
faking a dramatic fall is no problem—we're always doing that to get
the penalty kick. While I'm on the ground I make sure to rub some
paint on the side of my head and goggles so it looks like I've been
hit. All I can think to myself is: I'm finally having fun! I'm their stupid Iraqi! They're shooting at me, they hate me. They may be having
fun, but I'm having more fun! (83)

Any knowledgeable student of U.S. cultural history should be amazed
at the spectacle reproduced here. Although Wafaa Bilal came to the States
only in 1992, after just fifteen years in country he already managed to
channel what many historians agree is the mother root of all authentic
U.S. culture—of our theater, our music, and even of our nation's perpetu-
ally childlike sense of self. I'm speaking, of course, about that minstrel
tradition which arose out of slavery, spawned in white supremacist caricatures of African American behavior, and which was in turn mastered by
blacks themselves—in order to (as Ralph Ellison so memorably put it)
"change the joke and slip the yoke." By playing "the stupid Iraqi," Bilal
follows in the footsteps of the most influential artists this nation has ever
known, and, like them, he does so in order to maintain his sanity, to survive. As he himself summarizes:

The trigger of the gun keeps wildly clicking. The eye of the camera
keeps searching me out. But I have won. I have outsmarted them all.
I turn my phone off and lie down to get a little sleep, giddy with
exhaustion and the exultation of fooling my tormentors. They came
at me with machine guns firing, but they have not defeated me. I
have survived—I survived Digg Day. (84)

It may well be that some readers of this chapter—like Eric the shooter—
would question Bilal's actions that day. When the artist turns off the gun,
when he shucks and jives for the camera, isn't he counterfeiting? Doesn't
his art depend on the truth of blood, of pain—isn't his body on the line?

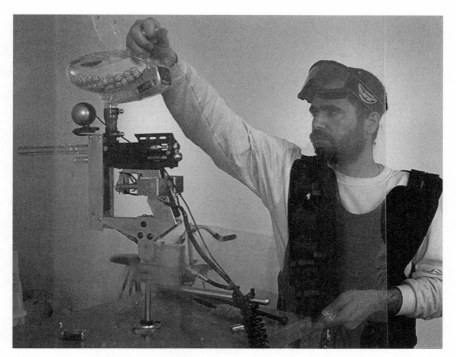

Domestic Tension, Wafaa Bilal loading the gun.

The first thing to remember, of course, is not to make a mystery of pain; the second thing is not to minimize the manic fervor of this moment. We need to recall that the near-insanity which Digg Day created wasn't an isolated incident; this reaction came from a man who had already survived violence in the home, confronted a murderous political regime, escaped the bombing of his hometown, and transformed one of the hellholes we reserve for refugees. We should wonder what would have become of us. Bilal's body is not all that the paintball project puts on the line, although it certainly does that too. It is Wafaa's sanity, it is, in a word, his humanity—and ours—that is first and foremost in play.

And once we've gotten that far, there is a last step to take. On Digg Day, as you will have noted, the enemy is clear—there can be no mistaking who is the aggressor. Torture, I have said, uses pain as an instrument, a limit case of how technology can reduce people to objects. "They will do with me what they want"; if a paving stone could talk, it would say no less. Meditating on the actions of Wafaa Bilal on that day, on his emotions, his intellect, and his actions, we eventually realize that he, like his brother Haji, had the courage to stay and face down a robotic and faceless foe. John Henry. No turning away, and no turning back.

And, FYI, the technology that enables a paintball gun to take orders off the Internet is in fact the same EZIO circuit board that allows cubicle warriors to operate Predator drones. In other words, the connection between these two events is no metaphor; it is literal. We must imagine Haji in his last moments, hypervigilant, staring fixedly at the black sky above, muttering to himself in rage, firing his machine gun blindly. Knowing what will happen, though not knowing when. The difference, of course, is that Wafaa's weapon of choice was his art. And he survives.

The experience of Digg Day stays with Bilal, as we imagine it must. One day, months later, as he watches a film starring Tom Hanks as a recycled Robinson Crusoe, Bilal comes to a deeper understanding of his experience in the gallery. The artist's reaction to this film ought to panic anyone who has ever felt isolated or trapped by our digitally mediated society (which is to say everyone). He summarizes its core elegantly:

> Tom Hanks' character becomes so desperate for companionship that he develops a deep friendship with a volleyball that also survived the crash. He paints a face on the ball with his own blood, attaches a shock of dry grass as hair and calls it Wilson, after the brand name emblazoned on the ball. He argues constantly with Wilson in an irascible one-way dialogue. When he loses Wilson after tossing him away in a fit of rage, he is devastated. (93)

Bilal then comments:

> I felt as though I were watching my relationship with the gun. I despised it, I cursed it, I never wanted to see or hear it again. But in that situation of isolation and stress, it was my steady companion, constantly alive and in motion. When it was silent, I felt lonely and abandoned. (93)

What both movie and artist describe is our human—and all-too-inhuman—propensity to worship those avatars that we ourselves create, or those that are thrust upon us. Confinement and isolation, whether behind a Facebook screen or within a gamer's world, opens the door to an uncanny, primordial animism. Some day soon, our desktops will talk back, and tell us to get a life.

With only a week left in his cell, Wafaa records a meditation on hope, a reflection based on records generated from his chat log. In the pages of *Shoot an Iraqi*, this is only the second time that the voices of his audience are cited at length—the other registers the vitriolic onslaught of hatred on Digg Day. The word "hope," Bilal notes, occurs in the log roughly 300 times. In some instances, the term betrays the very sentiment it expresses ("I hope your mother dies of vaginal cancer" [128]); other comments are, he notes, "pedestrian or indecipherable" ("Hope you're recycling"; "Hope someone builds an ark for this bible flood" [128]). Simple questions, or simple empathy, are also expressed as hopes. Bilal remembers as well that a number of messages register a hope for change, and, in the last instance, he himself mentions those that give him hope. Summing it up, he remarks, "Seeing how many people invoke hope in the chat room, I am convinced that it is not just empty rhetoric or my lofty idealism. Despite all that's wrong in the world, people do have hope. I feel lucky to have given them a platform to share it" (130). Glover would no doubt be pleased; hope is a currency we can safely call human.

As the month-long paintball project ends, a truly great, spontaneous irruption of hope takes shape in both behavior and language. With only a few days left in the project, during a dark hour in which the shooting has once again reached an unbearably high frequency, a former art student and watcher finds a way out. She realizes that the project's website controls can be used not just to target Wafaa, but also to protect him. By sending repeated commands to turn the gun to the left, she can manage to block the shooters, so long as her clicks outnumber theirs. She organizes others and, out of the watchers and shooters, a group of protectors is formed. They call themselves the Virtual Human Shield. Working together, they set up shifts and manage to shelter Wafaa for the duration. Rousseau's imprisoned man pushes at last on the door, only to find it has been unlocked all along.

In 1998, a couple of years after the wars in Bosnia and Croatia, and one before the NATO bombing of Belgrade, the Serbian writer David Albahari published a novel titled *Götz and Meyer*. This imaginative tour de force will serve as a final example, and a dramatic counterweight to *Kony 2012*. Albahari's text—a single paragraph of well over one hundred fifty pages—recounts the efforts of a Jewish schoolteacher in Belgrade to excavate the local World War II history that led to the murder of nearly all of his relatives. Most specifically, the protagonist attempts to imagine the lives and actions of the titular characters, two low-ranking SS officers who drove hundreds of prisoners from the Sajmište concentration camp outside of Belgrade—gassing them to death in the sealed compartment of their truck during transport, and supervising their burial in mass graves at Jajinci (site of perhaps eighty thousand Nazi victims).

On one of many occasions when the topic was discussed by the media, I remember asking my sister what she thought about having a Truth and Reconciliation–style commission for Bosnia-Herzegovina and the former Yugoslavia. "Yes," she replied, "it's a good idea. So long as they start with the Second World War." In Albahari's magisterial work, the more recent conflicts are never mentioned directly, yet it seems clear that the writer— who as chair of the Yugoslav Federation of Jewish Communities helped in organizing the evacuation of Jews from Sarajevo as the Bosnian war began— chose his subject in part as a response to the horrors of 1991–95. Seen in this light, the novel is itself a political act, a performative intervention into collective, national memory. At a time when the ICTY was more potential than actual (with many of those it had indicted for war crimes still in power or in hiding), Albahari's investigation aimed at portraying two war criminals from the inside, at reconstructing the daily routine of two apparently ordinary Germans, two men who also happened to commit unspeakable acts on a regular basis.[7] His schoolteacher is thus a researcher, both historian and judge—in short, an observer. Although he has little actual data to work with, this archival silence, if anything, seems simply to fuel his imperative, obsessive quest. Unlike Jason Russell and Invisible Children, Albahari's protagonist doesn't seek to make Götz and Meyer "famous," he simply tries to "look at [their] real faces" (167). In the book's final pages, the schoolteacher comments that "as long as their faces are nothing but a stand-in for any face, Götz and Meyer will return" (167). Both our lives and history itself, he adds, are made meaningless when that happens.

It seems fitting to end *Lessons from Sarajevo* with a tale told by a Yugoslav schoolteacher. The parallel in fact goes deeper: the climax of Albahari's novel itself stages a lesson—the schoolteacher ultimately decides he must take his students on a field trip, a "hands-on demonstration," to the sites of the Sajmište (i.e., "Fairgrounds") camp and the graves at Jajinci. As this trip unfolds, he assigns names from his list of relatives to each of the children:

> Each of you, I said, will now become someone else, each will become first the name, and then the person who bore that name. I began handing out names as if I were scattering seeds. The boys became my boy cousins, the girls my girl cousins. I gave them an age for each name, an occupation, real or imagined, sometimes hair color, density of eyebrows [. . .] Then I began a roll call, to turn them into little family groups, to arrange them in a column, and, though a little disorderly, they marched with even steps to the gate to the Fairgrounds camp. The bus was waiting, bathed in sunlight. The driver was asleep, resting his cheek on his arms folded over the steering wheel. As I called their names and as they got onto the bus, I told them they should imagine how the person whose name they carried entered the gray truck, whose dimensions I had repeated several times and which was driven by Götz and Meyer [. . .] I started to say the names, the bus filled slowly, the driver woke up, smacked his lips, and immediately began to whistle, the students' faces were grim, anxious, they were all silent, although the mothers touched the children, the husbands leaned over their wives, but all in silence, as if under water or at a very high altitude, in rarefied mountain air. Whatever it was, I found myself among my relatives, and I have no words to describe the sweetness I felt, that same way I felt when I hung the drawing of the family tree on the wall for the first time. (142–46)

In 1968, one day after the assassination of Martin Luther King, a schoolteacher named Jane Elliott concocted a similar "hands-on demonstration" in a small town in Iowa for her all-white class of third graders. In "A Class Divided," the PBS *Frontline* documentary commemorating this act of radical pedagogy, Elliott recalls her classroom that morning, and, in particular, one pupil who asked her, "Mrs. Elliott, why'd they shoot that King?":

> I knew from the night before that it was time to deal with this in a concrete way, and not just talk about it. We had talked about racism since the first day of school. But the shooting of Martin Luther King, who had been one of our heroes of the month in February, could not just be talked about and explained away. There was no way to explain this to a little third grader in Riceville, Iowa.

Instead of explaining, Elliott divided up her class into two groups: blue-eyed children and brown-eyed children, and set up a series of rules privileging one group and discriminating against the other. The next day, she reversed her social rigging. As in Albahari's novel, the children had no trouble at all falling into their roles, and the results were disquieting, to say the least.

In *Götz and Meyer*, however, the schoolteacher's lesson doesn't lend itself to reversals. Albahari's story continues:

> The truck stopped two or three times, but it started up again soon, and then someone recognized by the sound that they were crossing the bridge. They were going back, at last, to Belgrade. Then just when they began to try and guess which streets they were driving along, the truck stopped. The people whose names you bear fell silent, I said, and then they listened tensely in the dark. They heard voices, recognized German, but none of them understood the words, then the door slammed, someone walked along the truck, went back, stood, you heard some sort of rattling on the floor, and as if that had been some predetermined signal, everyone began to speak at once, to shout and bang the sides of the truck, until the door to the cab slammed again and the engine started up [. . .] soon after that second start, the people whose names you bear began to notice the smell of fuel exhaust. At first it was pleasant, like some secret bond with the outside world, and then more and more repellent, but sweetish, followed by nausea, a powerful headache, choking, hoarse screams, although there were those who lowered their heads and fell asleep. I

touched my lips to the head on the microphone and looked at the students. Most of them were straining to breathe, one girl had clutched her throat, someone's hand struggled feebly toward the window and then slid helplessly back, one boy covered his eyes with his hands, two girls had their arms round each other, their heads on one another's shoulders, I saw some lips moving, but except for the driver's soft whistling I heard no sounds. (147–49)

To quote at length, as I have here, the climax of *Götz and Meyer* may actually be somewhat misleading, and even appear to contradict my summary of the novel's aim, that goal which gives the book its title—a character sketch of two SS officers presenting them as both human and criminal. In the quoted passages, it seems clear, the focus is instead on communicating the experience of the victims, not the executioners. And the lesson learned is that history is a nightmare.

And yet things aren't so simple. In order to teach this lesson, Albahari's schoolteacher must himself become more than a researcher; he must assume the role of the Germans. After all, as in Iowa, this hands-on demonstration is proposed, performed, and controlled by the schoolteacher; in order to learn what sort of world we live in, the pupils are forced to play out a rigged game, a representation that is not just history, but art. Think of Whitman's wound-dresser, removing bandages for that soldier who "dares not look on the bloody stump, / And has not yet look'd on it." The schoolteachers, in both cases, dictate and impose a societal simulacrum in which racist violence holds sway—yet they do so to cut out disease, and heal wounds.

To complicate things further, in the Albahari at least, a categorical difference between real war and books is also made explicit. When asked what they would bring with them, if they had to leave their homes forever, the Serb children list an entire menagerie of animals that they refuse to leave behind. When told that the rules clearly prohibit such things, a girl in the class exclaims, "Why, this is inhuman" (131). And at this point, the schoolteacher pounces:

That is the difference I want to talk about, the fact that you keep imagining reality as if it were an artwork in which you have a choice,

> while in the tangible world there is no choice, you have to partici-
> pate, you cannot step out of what is going on and into something
> else, there is nothing else except what is going on, whether you like
> it or not, and that means you must feel the cold taking over, and you
> must have at least an inkling that you will never be back, and that
> you will never see your pets again, and that your rooms, as you left
> them, will soon be entered by people for whom none of your memen-
> tos, none of those little things you fuss over, will mean anything.
> (131)

Harsh as this lesson is, it remains only a lesson; the students are asked to
imagine a reality in which they have no choice. That they choose to do so
is itself a form of art, an attempt to both approximate and intervene in the
very history they inherit.[8]

During the field trip from Belgrade, a particular choice makes this difference in categories literally inescapable. In his attempt to make concrete
what took place on this very soil a half century earlier, the schoolteacher
happens upon a puzzling, and ultimately telling, move. He invents a character: a child named Adam, only thirteen, preparing for a bar mitzvah;
none of his relatives in the camp fit this description. Adam appears to be
the age of his students, yet when it comes time to assign a name to each of
the passengers in the bus, the schoolteacher reserves Adam for himself.

And it doesn't end there. This invented character, as the schoolteacher
imagines him, somehow manages to anticipate the fate awaiting his fellow prisoners. He even steals a gas mask, hides it under his shirt, and uses
it to survive the transport to Jajinci. When the truck arrives, he reaches the
door, climbing over the corpses of the other Jews. Yet he is then shot by a
German soldier. The schoolteacher comments:

> Adam was dead. I'd thought, I'd hoped he would survive. I could
> have lain down between the bus seats and fallen asleep instantly, I
> was so drained. It isn't easy to show someone that the world, like a
> sock, has its other side, and that all you need is one skillful twist to
> switch one side to the other, skillful and quick, so that no one
> notices the change, but everyone accepts that the wrong side is in
> fact the right side of the world. (159)

Out of the entire lesson, however, it is the story of Adam that sinks in; the fate of this invented soul worries three of the girls in the class. When they inquire of the schoolteacher if souls can be lost, he replies, "Of course they can [. . .] although a soul that remembers can never be lost." "Don't all souls remember?" they ask. "Some of them don't," he answers, "some try to forget" (160). This response satisfies them—apparently they have decided not to side with oblivion. Later, to himself, the schoolteacher adds,

> as long as there is remembering, that was what I had really wanted to say to them, there is a chance, no matter how slim, that someone, once, somewhere, will look at the real faces of Götz and Meyer, something I hadn't managed to do. And as long as their faces are nothing but a stand-in for any face, Götz and Meyer will return and repeat the meaninglessness of history that becomes, in the end, the meaninglessness of our lives. (167)

All this is, of course, a far cry from the clear and simple, sentimental, even childlike message of *Kony 2012*: Joseph Kony is a very very bad man; he must be stopped and brought to justice. And yet, given that—as Nicholas Kristof and HRW note—the message of *Kony 2012* does have the minor virtue of truth, what then makes the complex and troubling story of *Götz and Meyer*—or those of Coetzee and Bilal for that matter—more suitable for the twenty-first century? Today viable ethical positions or political solutions are unlikely to be found by five-year-olds—in other words, by our chimp brains. Instead, we'll need the complex thinking of artists like these to identify and explore our social rigging, whether historical, actual, or potential. It would do a disservice to these rich, complex, and nuanced stories to reduce their strengths to a sound-bite conclusion. Their common goal, on the other hand, is simple: keep the devil way down in the hole.

As the second millennium was whimpering its way to an end, the French political philosopher Jacques Rancière wrote that true change comes only in rare moments of history. The rest of the time, he told us, is mostly a matter of mopping up, of maintaining the social order as is, of policing its borders. Within every society, according to this view from afar, there is a fixed distribution of goods, of power, and of language. The business of most days, and most eras, is to make sure that what is fixed stays fixed.

Each society, Rancière also believes, has a part of its population that is without goods and without power—and these poor souls are thought to be without language as well. Change in history comes (and it does come) on that rare day when those who are left behind demand to be heard. They do so by mastering the language of their masters, and turning it against them.[9]

I simply don't know whether our time is one of those times, whether today is a moment in which the voiceless and oppressed will rise up and demand their fair share of the wealth of this world. Most moments in history, I'm guessing, have been able to make either argument about their place in history. All that was solid—one side cries—has melted into air. Everything that rises must converge, replies the other. We do know, as Carlo Ginzburg stirringly reminds us, that some things surely have changed, that our power to destroy the future may some day irrevocably rewrite our past. We had better keep our ears to the ground.

Waiting for the Barbarians, Shoot an Iraqi, and *Götz and Meyer,* it should be clear, are similar in that each of their stories refuses a fixed disposition of roles, one that found its modern form some three centuries ago. Like Coetzee's magistrate, or Albahari's schoolteacher, Wafaa Bilal's performance piece moves the artist through each of the positions that sentimental forms of representation freeze in place—victim, aggressor, observer. The artist as target, the objectification and suffering of his body and mind, are where he chooses to place himself. But he also loads the gun, and even creates the very mechanism that allows it to be aimed. Finally, as any artist must, he also stands outside the work, in front of its dynamic, shifting scene, making those choices which in part determine what we see.

For the twenty-first century, or at least for now, such narratives offer us a pretty good rule of thumb. War stories today should be judged on whether, and to what extent, they deny us the easy way out, and make it impossible for us to see the positions of victim, aggressor, and observer as immutable, assigned in advance. Coetzee's magistrate understands that his own history is unlikely to allow him to crack the code of those whose lives and languages his kind have so long failed to recognize. But that doesn't stop him from trying, and he may perhaps be bettered by the attempt. Albahari's schoolteacher fails to unlock the identity of two men who remain resistantly ordinary, and unspeakably evil. And yet he may have managed to sow the seeds of memory and thus "prevent the weeds of forgetting from growing" (167). For a month in the spring of 2007, Wafaa Bilal's lifelong project of bringing war stories home held up the shield of Perseus and allowed us to see the lived experience—the material meaning—of war. Medusa, as we know, lives on.

Notes

1. Case Study: Of Phantom Nations

1. In recent years, there has been a veritable explosion of related work, in at least four distinct fields. A very partial list would include, in philosophy, the work of Akeel Bilgrami, Martha Nussbaum, and Amélie O. Rorty; in affect theory, that of Sara Ahmed, Lauren Berlant, Judith Butler, and Eve K. Sedgwick; in trauma studies, that of Nicolas Abraham and Maria Torok, Cathy Caruth, and Dominick LaCapra; and in literary history, Nancy Armstrong, Margaret Doody, and Janet Todd. In the discussion that follows, as well as in chapter 2, only the barest tips of these several icebergs will be seen.

2. The website for the Smithsonian American Art Museum displays this letter in a slideshow presentation of the building's history, called "Temple of Invention. History of a National Landmark": www.npg.si.edu/exhibit/pob/index.html.

3. *Oxford English Dictionary, s.v.* "convulsion" and "convulsiveness" (954, 955).

4. Well, not entirely. In fact, the phantom arm disappeared, but the hand did not—it remains present to this day, felt as if it were attached directly to the shoulder where the patient's amputation occurred. This bizarre phenomenon Ramachandran refers to as the "telescoping" of the phantom (as in closing a telescope); he has observed it in other patients as well. The neuroscientist speculates that the persistence of the hand as phantom is due to the greater relative importance of the sensory information sent by that appendage to the brain.

5. Ramachandran: "How does this illusory feeling happen? When you move your hand, motor command centers in the front of the brain send a signal out, down the spinal cord to the muscles on the opposite side of the body. At the same time, a copy of the command (like an email cc) goes to the parietal lobe [. . .] [T]his area gets both visual and proprioceptive (body-position sense) feedback that can be compared with the motor command, thereby forming a feedback loop to ensure accuracy. If the arm is lost, there is no proprioceptive feedback, but the copy of the command is nonetheless sent to the parietal lobe and sensed by the patient's brain as movements of the phantom" (17).

2. Thesis: The Crime of the Scene

1. See, for example, the following studies: Charaudeau, *La télévision et la guerre*; Gow, Paterson, and Preston, *Bosnia by Television*; and Sadkovich, *The U.S. Media and Yugoslavia, 1991–1995*.

2. To my knowledge, the first use of this passage—which has since become something of a touchstone—to unpack the historical import of sentimentalism can be found in "Making a Thing into a Man: The Sentimental Novel and Slavery," from Philip Fisher's *Hard Facts* (87–127).

3. It did occur to me that Rousseau could conceivably have been engaged here in a philosophical form of hostile takeover, attempting, in other words, to turn Mandeville's satire into support for his own cause. Mandeville does grant that even criminals feel sympathy, though he uses that admission to expose the ineffectiveness of benevolence itself—a criminal is still a criminal, despite his heart of gold. For Rousseau, what is essential is that sympathy (and not only greed or self-preservation) can be seen as common to all humankind, and beyond.

4. Just what irony might look like in a war photo seemed puzzling to me, until I recalled another of Haviv's photos. In this shot, a middle-aged soldier with a rifle rides a bicycle past a burning house, looking directly at the photographer and waving. When I show this photo in class, my students are generally confused by it, and occasionally they come up with some rather bizarre and inventive explanations for what it represents. They need to be told, of course, that the soldier is a member of the Serb paramilitary force which must have set the home on fire, and that his salute to the photographer is a nationalist sign, not the peace symbol or a V for victory. They are amused, in any case, both by his age and by the fact that he's riding a woman's bike.

5. This story, first reported by Elizabeth Drew of the *Washington Post*, has since been very widely circulated. See, for example, Drew's book *On the Edge: The Clinton Presidency*, as well as an article by Jason De Parle in the *New York Times* ("The Man Inside Bill Clinton's Foreign Policy," August 20, 1995) and Yahya Sadowski in the *London Guardian* ("The Big Extract: What Really Makes the World Go to War," August 1, 1998). In his career as pundit, Kaplan often takes positions diametrically opposed to those his own book appears to suggest. In the transcript of a CNN program on June 9, 1995, the host, Judy Woodruff, and Sen. Dan Coats (R-Ind.) each virtually summarize Kaplan's book; Kaplan himself, in contrast, takes his distance from both, siding instead with Sen. Joseph Lieberman. Recent editions of *Balkan Ghosts* also contain a foreword in which Kaplan himself discusses the issue.

6. "Largely written before" would be a more accurate statement. In addition to the foreword, the prologue, and the preface, there are a number of footnotes containing dates and references to events in the former Yugoslavia which postdate the outbreak of hostilities. How much else in Kaplan's opening chapters was also rewritten is unclear, although a number of passages do appear to have been added.

7. This work is found in Sarhandi and Boboc, *Evil Doesn't Live Here*.

3. Victims: The Talking Dead

1. My summary of the thesis of Jacques Rancière's seminal work, *La mésentente: Politique et philosophie.*

2. The Library of Congress has an excellent website that offers free access to many Brady studio photographs: http://memory.loc.gov/ammem/cwphtml/cwphome. html.

3. "The Dead in this War—there they lie, strewing the fields and woods and valleys and battle-fields of the South—Virginia, the Peninsula—Malvern Hill and Fair Oaks—the banks of the Chickahominy—the terraces of Fredericksburgh—Antietam bridge—the grisly ravines of Manassas—the bloody promenade of the Wilderness—the varieties of the *strayed* dead, (the estimate of the War Department is 25,000 National soldiers kill'd in battle and never buried at all, 5,000 drown'd—15,000 inhumed strangers or on the march in haste, in hitherto unfound localities—2,000 graves cover'd by sand and mud, by Mississippi freshets, 3,000 carried away by caving-in of banks, &c.,)—Gettysburgh, the West, Southwest—Vicksburg—Chattanooga—the trenches of Petersburgh—the numberless battles, camps, Hospitals everywhere"(*Memoranda* 102).

4. Although there may be a family resemblance, irony as deployed by Fussell is only a distant cousin to its description in chapter 2. In Mandeville, ironic distancing is used to deconstruct the foolishness of those who, like Rousseau, would believe in humanity. In war as Fussell tells it, the distance between our beliefs and the facts on the ground is delivered by history itself. Memory too becomes a function of this distance: the soldier recalls only odd, absurd, or futile juxtapositions between our actions and actuality—"a slaughter by itself is too commonplace for notice" (31). All the writer of war stories can do, Fussell argues, is search for an objective form that correlates to the events surrounding him. Irony, both mindset and verbal sleight-of-hand, is his modus operandi.

5. Some writers have made this tendency toward the increased targeting of civilians appear more simple than it likely is: see Roberts, "Lives and Statistics," as well as Gutman and Rieff, *Crimes of War.*

6. A couple of jokes, then. Here's one that nearly everybody there used to know. Q. How do they give directions in Banja Luka? A. Turn left where the mosque used to be.

   Too quick? Let me try another one. Mujo is walking down the street, just out of the hospital after having his right arm amputated. He's depressed to the point of desperation, crying, talking to himself, thinking about suicide. He can't bear the thought of life without his arm. Suddenly he sees Suljo walking toward him, skipping and smiling. When he gets closer, Mujo sees that Suljo is actually laughing out loud. What is most amazing to Mujo is that Suljo is carrying on like this despite the fact that, not just one, but *both* of his arms have been amputated.

   So Mujo stops Suljo, who continues to snicker and smile. Mujo says, "Suljo, I don't understand you. I'm desperate, I'm even thinking about killing myself, all because I've had one arm amputated. You've had both your arms cut off and here you are smiling and laughing like an idiot. In your condition, how can you be so happy?"

Suljo replies, "Mujo, if you'd had both of your arms cut off, like I did, and your ass was itching like crazy, like mine is, you'd be laughing too."

7. Originally published in the Bosnian weekly *Dani*, this translation of Mehmedinovic''s review is given on the Charming Hostess website (http://charminghostess.us/dani.html).

4. Observers: The Real War and the Books

1. "Tant qu'il n'y aura pas de cinéma olfactif comme il y a un cinéma parlant, il n'y aura pas de films de guerre, ce qui est d'ailleurs prudent, parce qu'à ce moment là, je vous jure bien qu'il n'y aura plus de spectateurs." From Eric Loret's review of Sacco in *Liberation*, January 25, 2001 (my translation).

2. For more information, see www.cla.purdue.edu/history/facstaff/ingrao/si/prospectus.pdf.

3. The full text can be found on the ICTY site at www.icty.org/sid/7941.

4. Just for the record, these images were filmed at Trnopolje, not Omarska itself. At the latter camp, the reporters were not even allowed to take pictures. The quotations from the Deichmann article which follow were downloaded in mid-December 2002.The article (as it appeared on December 13, 2002) has been archived at http://web.archive.org/web/20021213160924/http://www.terravista.pt/guincho/2104/199810/deichmann_9701.html.

5. Again, just for the record, here is a brief quotation from the first British newspaper account about the camps:

> Trnopolje camp, down another 10 miles of dirt road, is claimed by the Muslim government to be the second biggest 'concentration camp.' Here, Muslim doctors among the internees said people arrived from Omarska and another 'investigation centre' at Kereter [i.e., Keraterm] in terrible condition. Evidence was passed to the *Guardian* and ITN in the form of a roll of undeveloped film.
>
> Here is complete confusion—political and physical. The camp is a ramshackle fenced-in compound around a former school. The men stand stripped to the waist, in their thousands, against the wire in the relentless afternoon heat the women and children seek shade upstairs in the crowded, smelly building. They wait, stare at nothing, sweat— and wonder what will happen next.
>
> One group has arrived from Kereter that morning, claiming that they had been beaten, but showing no signs of it. However, says pitifully thin Fikrit Alic: 'It is worse than here. There is no food.' Others in the group looked better fed. Another boy, Icic Budo, says 'they killed 200 people'

at Kereter and 'many more at Omarska'. He has seen no bodies himself, but another boy had seen one corpse near the main gate.

Trnopolje cannot be called a 'concentration camp' and is nowhere as sinister as Omarska: it is very grim, something between a civilian prison and transit camp. The Yugoslav Red Cross has a small station here, and there are meagre cooking facilities. (Ed Vulliamy, *Guardian*, April 7, 1992)

After ITN won its court case against LM, Vulliamy added the following reflections:

At the time I paid little attention to what would become *Living Marxism*'s myopic obsessions: such as which side of which pole the old barbed wire or fresh barbed wire was fixed. There were more important matters, such as the emaciated Fikret Alic's (accurate and vindicated) recollections of the night he had been assigned to load the bodies of 250 men killed in one night at yet another camp.

If it is still of any remote interest, I will say this: I now know the compound in which these terrified men were held captive to have been surrounded on one side by recently reinforced barbed wire, on two sides by a chain-link fence patrolled by menacing armed thugs and on a fourth side by a wall. But so what? This was a camp—I would say a concentration camp—and they were its inmates. (Vulliamy, *Guardian*, March 15, 2000)

6. The obvious bears repeating on another point as well. As Elie Wiesel comments, in his preface to a memoir from an Omarska survivor, "Omarska was not Auschwitz. Nothing, anywhere, can be compared to Auschwitz. But what took place at Omarska was sufficient [. . .] to justify international intervention and international solidarity" (Hukanović vii). As for Fikret Alić, the shirtless man left of center in Deichmann's photo, the LM article originally claimed that his horribly emaciated state was due to "a childhood bout of tuberculosis" (Connolly). This claim no longer appears in online versions of Deichmann's article. David Campbell has written a detailed critique of Deichmann's article and an analysis of this media controversy and its political implications in the *Journal of Human Rights*.

7. Calvino's retelling of the Perseus story is suggestive in other ways as well. The Italian author does confess that he is tempted "to see this myth as an allegory on the poet's relationship to the world," but he also argues that "any interpretation impoverishes the myth and suffocates it" (4). His reluctance to succumb to this temptation is, in part, a reluctance to see himself simply as Perseus. In one instance, he actually identifies more closely with Andromeda; after all, the heroic "Perseus comes to his aid" as well (4). Moreover, by stressing that Perseus carries Medusa's head as "his particular burden," Calvino also suggests that his hero's "delicacy of spirit" (5) contains and controls the "savage horror of the Gorgon" (6). Her power, to turn enemies to stone, is now his.

8. Much of my discussion is based on sources found at the *American Memory* website of the Library of Congress Prints and Photographs Division: http://memory.loc

.gov/ammem/cwphtml/cwphome.html. The quotations from Alexander Gardner's *Photographic Sketch Book* can be found there as well.

9. Perhaps the most sustained and thoughtful examination of these issues can be found in the work of Dominick LaCapra, much of which is in direct dialogue with White. See, for example, his *Writing History, Writing Trauma*.

10. Insofar as it attempts to capture "an order of experience beyond (or prior to) [. . .] the kinds of opposition we are forced to draw (between agency and patiency, subjectivity and objectivity, literalness and figurativeness, fact and fiction, history and myth, and so forth) in any version of realism" (White 39).

5. Aggressors: The Beast Is Back

1. "War is beautiful even though it hurts." (The last phrase could also be translated "causes pain" or even "does evil.") The quote comes from the song "Generale," on his 1978 album *De Gregori*.

2. Miranda: "O, wonder! / How many goodly creatures are there here! / How beauteous mankind is! O brave new world / That hath such people in't!" Prospero: "'Tis new to thee" (*The Tempest*, 5.1.181–84).

3. This insistent attention to one set of artists, and blindness to a more obvious and much wider field within Western visual culture, for Eisenman, is evidence of an "Abu Ghraib effect," a Freudian parapraxis which has largely succeeded in repressing the uncanny doubling between these most recent documents of Western barbarism and some of the "most familiar and beloved images" in its representational tradition.

4. One of the more extensive discussions of Limbaugh's comments within the mainstream media was given by Dick Meyer on CBSnews.com: www.cbsnews .com/stories/2004/05/06/opinion/meyer/main616021.shtml. See as well the comments by Kurt Nimmo at www.pressaction.com/news/weblog/full_article/ nimmo05082004/. References to the remarks can also be found in columns by Maureen Dowd ("Shocking and Awful," *New York Times*, May 6, 2004) and Frank Rich ("Saving Private England," *New York Times*, May 16, 2004).

5. In his brilliant short story "Walk with Us," Askold Melnyczuk confronts this split-brain reaction directly, inventing a narrator who is the mother of a U.S. soldier closely resembling Lynndie England.

6. In a *New York Times* essay written only a few days after the photos became public, Luc Sante called them precisely that. He also saw a resemblance between the attitudes they displayed and the photographic records of crowds at lynchings.

7. See www.ejumpcut.org/archive/jc47.2005/links.html.

8. By the end of his conversations with Verbitsky, Scilingo no longer uses these official euphemisms for the state policies of kidnapping, torture, and murder (154).

9. The phrase in quotes is from President Menem (Verbitsky 15).

Conclusion: Bringing the Stories Home

1. Richard A. Oppel Jr., "Strikes in Pakistan Underscore Obama's Options," *New York Times*, January 23, 2009.

2. First aired on January 30, 2009, both video and transcript are available on the program's website, www.pbs.org/moyers/journal/01302009/profile.html.

3. First aired on April 8, 2008, this interview can be heard online at www.npr.org/templates/story/story.php?storyId=89460867.

4. This show first aired on January 22, 2009; the interview can be heard online at www.npr.org/templates/story/story.php?storyId=99663723.

5. On the "cold joke" and its prevalence in combat situations, see Glover, *Humanity*.

6. This episode from Bilal's biography has been illustrated by the graphic artist Summer McClinton. See Bilal and Lyderson, "Gulf War."

7. In a note at the end of the novel, Albahari notes two sources in particular for his work, and one is an article by Christopher Browning, "The Final Solution in Serbia: The Judenlager at the Fairgrounds" (published in Serbian in *Zbornik* 6, SJOJ, Belgrade, 1992). Browning's best-known work is *Ordinary Men: Reserve Police Battalion 101 and the Final Solution in Poland* (New York: HarperCollins, 1992).

8. Whether children in the former Yugoslavia in fact receive similar lessons, or whether they instead imbibe the heady nationalism of the *génocidaires* is an open question. Dubravka Ugrešić's "Old Men and Their Grandchildren" argues that the latter case may in fact be the majority position.

9. This summary is intended to recapitulate the argument of Rancière's *La mésentente*.

Works Cited

Abumrad, Jad, and Robert Krulwich. "Morality." *Radiolab* 2.3 (August 13, 2007). www.radiolab.org/2007/aug/13/.

Albahari, David. *Götz and Meyer*. Trans. E. Elias-Bursac. New York: Harcourt, 2006.

Améry, Jean. *At the Mind's Limits: Contemplations by a Survivor on Auschwitz and Its Realities*. Trans. S. Rosenfeld and S. P. Rosenfeld. Bloomington: Indiana University Press, 1980.

Anderson, Benedict. *Imagined Communities: Reflections on the Origin and Spread of Nationalism*. New York: Verso, 2006.

Andrić, Ivo. *The Bridge on the Drina*. Trans. L. F. Edwards. Intro. W. H. McNeill. Chicago: University of Chicago Press, 1977.

Arendt, Hannah. *On Revolution*. Westport, CT: Greenwood Press, 1963.

———. *The Human Condition*. Chicago: University of Chicago Press, 1958.

Bašić, Adisa. "Trauma Market." Trans. Una Tanović. *Massachusetts Review* 52.3/4 (2011): 721.

Berman, Marshall. *All That Is Solid Melts into Air: The Experience of Modernity*. New York: Simon & Schuster, 1982.

Bilal, Wafaa, and Kari Lydersen. *Shoot an Iraqi: Art, Life, and Resistance under the Gun*. San Francisco: City Lights, 2008.

———. "Gulf War: Portrait of the Artist as a Refugee." With art by Summer McClinton. *Massachusetts Review* 52.3/4 (2011): 756–61.

Breton André. *Manifestoes of Surrealism*. Trans. R. Seaver and H. Lane. Ann Arbor: University of Michigan Press, 1972.

Calvino, Italo. *The Path to the Nest of Spiders*. Trans. A. Coloquhoun. New York: Ecco Press, 1976.

———. *Six Memos for the Next Millenium*. Trans. P. Creagh. Cambridge: Harvard University Press, 1988.

Campbell, David. "Atrocity, Memory, Photography: Imaging the Concentration
    Camps of Bosnia—The Case of ITN versus *Living Marxism*, Part 1."
    Journal of Human Rights 1.1 (2002): 1–33.
————. "Atrocity, Memory, Photography: Imaging the Concentration Camps of
    Bosnia—The Case of ITN versus *Living Marxism*, Part 2." *Journal of
    Human Rights* 1.2 (2002): 143–72.
Caruth, Cathy. "The Wound and the Voice." In *Unclaimed Experience: Trauma, Narra-
    tive, and History*, 1–9. Baltimore: Johns Hopkins University Press, 1996.
Cast Away. Dir. Robert Zemeckis. Perf. Tom Hanks, Helen Hunt, Paul Sanchez.
    Twentieth Century Fox, 2000.
Charaudeau, Patrick. *La télévision et la guerre: Déformation ou construction de la réalité?
    Le conflit en Bosnie (1990–1994)*. Louvain-la-Neuve: Ina-De Boeck, 2001.
A Class Divided. PBS Frontline. Dir. William Peters. Written by William Peters and
    Charlie Cobb. March 26, 1985.
Cohen, Roger. *Hearts Grown Brutal: Sagas of Sarajevo*. New York: Random House,
    1998.
Coetzee, J. M. *Diary of a Bad Year*. New York: Viking, 2008.
————. *Waiting for the Barbarians*. New York: Penguin, 1999.
Connolly, Kate "The Face of Bosnia's Civil War." http://observer.guardian.
    co.uk/milosevic/story/0,,769071,00.html.
De Man, Paul. "The Rhetoric of Blindness." In *Blindness and Insight*, 102–41.
    Minneapolis: University of Minnesota Press.
Deichmann, Thomas. "The Picture That Fooled the World." *Living Marxism*.
    Archived as it appeared on December 13, 2002, at http://web.archive
    .org/web/20021213160924/http://www.terravista.pt/guincho/2104
    /199810/deichmann_9701.html.
Demick, Barbara. *Logavina Street: Life and Death in a Sarajevo Neighborhood*. Kansas
    City, MO: Andrews & McMeel, 1996.
Dobyns, Kenneth W. *The Patent Office Pony: A History of the Early Patent Office*.
    Fredericksburg, VA: Sergeant Kirkland's Museum and Historical
    Society, 1994. www.myoutbox.net/pohome.htm.
Doody, Margaret Anne. *A Natural Passion: A Study of the Novels of Samuel Richardson*.
    Oxford: Clarendon Press, 1974.
Doubt, Keith. *Sociology after Bosnia and Kosovo*. Lanham, MD: Rowman &
    Littlefield, 2000.

Drew, Elizabeth. *On the Edge: The Clinton Presidency.* New York: Simon & Schuster, 1994.

Ellis, John B. *The Sight and Secrets of the National Capital: A Work Descriptive of Washington City in All Its Various Phases.* New York: United States Publishing Company, 1869.

Eisenman, Stephen. *The Abu Ghraib Effect.* London: Reaktion, 2007.

FAMA International. *Sarajevo Survival Map.* www.sa92.ba/v1/index. php?showimage=259.

———. *Sarajevo Survival Guide.* (See under Prstojević et al.)

Filipović, Zlata. *Zlata's Diary.* London: Penguin, 1994.

Fisher, Philip. *Hard Facts: Setting and Form in the American Novel.* New York: Oxford University Press, 1985.

Frassanito, William. *Gettysburg: A Journey in Time.* New York: Scribner, 1975.

Freud, Sigmund. *Beyond the Pleasure Principle.* New York: Norton, 1989.

Friedlander, Saul, ed. *Probing the Limits of Representation.* Cambridge: Harvard University Press, 1992.

Fussell, Paul. *The Great War and Modern Memory.* New York: Oxford University Press, 1975.

Geertz, Clifford. *The Interpretation of Cultures.* New York: Basic, 1973.

Ginzburg, Carlo. "Killing a Chinese Mandarin." In *Historical Change and Human Rights: The Oxford Amnesty Lectures, 1994,* edited by Olwen Hufton, 55–74. New York: Basic, 1995.

Gjelten, Tom. *Sarajevo Daily: A City and Its Newspaper under Siege.* New York: HarperCollins, 1995.

Glover, Jonathan. *Humanity: A Moral History of the Twentieth Century.* New Haven: Yale Univerity Press, 2000.

Gorman, Erna Blitzer. *While Other Children Played: A Hidden Child Remembers the Holocaust.* Ed. B. J. Kriigel. Dearborn: University of Michigan–Dearborn, 2010.

Gourevitch, Philip. *We Wish to Inform You That Tomorrow We Will Be Killed with Our Families: Stories from Rwanda.* New York: Farrar, Straus & Giroux, 1998.

Gourevitch, Philip, and Errol Morris. *Standard Operating Procedure.* New York: Penguin, 2008.

Gow, James, Richard Paterson, and Alison Preston, eds. *Bosnia by Television.* London: British Film Institute, 1996.

The Green Berets. Dir. John Wayne and Ray Kellogg. Perf. John Wayne, David
     Janssen, Jim Hutton. Warner Bros/Seven Arts, 1968.

Green, Joshua D., et al. "An fMRI Investigation of Emotional Engagement in
     Moral Judgment." *Science* 293 (2001): 2105–8.

———. "The Neural Bases of Cognitive Conflict and Control in Moral
     Judgment." *Neuron* 44 (2004): 389–400.

Gutman, Roy, and David Rieff, eds. *Crimes of War: What the Public Should Know.*
     New York: Norton, 1999.

Hanley, Lynn. *Writing War: Fiction, Gender, and Memory.* Amherst: University of
     Massachusetts Press, 1991.

Haviv, Ron. *Blood and Honey: A Balkan War Journal.* Essays by C. Sudetic and
     D. Rieff. Afterword B. Kouchner. New York: TV Books, 2000.

Herr, Michael. *Dispatches.* New York: Avon, 1977.

Hukanović, Rezak. *The Tenth Circle of Hell.* Intro. E. Wiesel. New York: Abacus, 1998.

Human Rights Watch. *Getting Away with Torture? The Bush Administration and the
     Mistreatment of Detainees.* www.hrw.org/reports/2011/07/12/
     getting-away-torture-0.

Hume, David. *A Treatise of Human Nature.* Ed. D. Norton and M. Norton. Intro.
     D. Norton. New York: Oxford University Press, 2000.

Ignatieff, Michael. *Virtual War: Kosovo and Beyond.* New York: Holt, 2000.

Illich, Ivan. H_2o *and the Waters of Forgetfulness.* London: Boyars, 1986.

Jacobs, Harriet A. *Incidents in the Life of a Slave Girl, Written by Herself.* Boston:
     Bedford, 2010.

Kaplan, Robert D. *Balkan Ghosts: A Journey through History.* New York: St. Martin's,
     1993.

Kebo, Ozren. *Bienvenue au enfer: Sarajevo mode d'emploi.* Trans. Mireille Robin.
     Paris: La Nuée Bleue, 1997.

Kony 2012. Dir. Jason Russell. Distributed by Invisible Children, Inc. Released
     March 5, 2012. www.youtube.com/watch?v=Y4MnpzG5Sqc.

Kristof, Nicholas D. "Viral Video, Vicious Warlord." *New York Times*, March 14,
     2012.

LaCapra, Dominick. *Writing History, Writing Trauma.* Baltimore: Johns Hopkins
     University Press, 2001.

Lacoue-Labarthe, Philippe, and Jean-Luc Nancy. "The Nazi Myth." *Critical Inquiry*
     16.2 (Winter 1990): 291–312.

Latour, Bruno. *War of the Worlds: What about Peace?* Chicago: Prickly Paradigm Press, 2002.

———. *We Have Never Been Modern.* Trans. C. Porter. Cambridge: Harvard University Press, 1993.

———. "Why Has Critique Run Out of Steam? From Matters of Fact to Matters of Concern." *Critical Inquiry* 30 (2004): 225–48.

Lehrer, Jonah. *Proust Was a Neuroscientist.* New York: Houghton Mifflin Harcourt, 2007.

Loret, Eric. "Tu n'a rien vu à Gorazde." *Libération*, January 25, 2001. www.liberation.fr/livres/0101361575-tu-n-as-rien-vu-a-gorazde.

Maass, Peter. *Love Thy Neighbor: A Story of War.* New York: Knopf, 1996.

Malcolm, Noel. "The Roots of Bosnian Horror Lie Not So Deep" (review of *Hearts Grown Brutal: Sagas of Sarajevo*, by Roger Cohen). *New York Times*, October 19, 1998.

Mandeville, Bernard de. *The Fable of the Bees.* Ed. F. B. Kaye. Oxford: Clarendon Press, 1924.

Mayer, Jane. "A Deadly Interrogation: Can the C.I.A. Legally Kill a Prisoner?" *New Yorker*, November 14, 2005.

McGuirk, Carol. "The Sentimental Encounter in Sterne, Mackenzie, and Burns." *Studies in English Literature, 1800–1900* 20.3 (1980): 505–15.

Mehmedinović, Semezdin. *Sarajevo Blues.* Trans. A. Alcalay. San Francisco: City Lights, 1998.

———. "The Devil and the Rose." Trans. J. Hicks. *Massachusetts Review* 50.3 (2009): 285–87.

Melnyczuk, Askold. "Walk with Us." *Massachusetts Review* 52.3/4 (2011): 477–88.

MGM Sarajevo: Man, God, and Monster. Dir. Pjer Žaljica, Mirza Idrizović, Ismet Arnautalić, and Ademir Kenović. Perf. Izudin Bajrović, Sead Bejtović, Ines Fanćović. SaGA Films, 1992–94.

Mitchell, S. Weir. "The Case of George Dedlow." *Atlantic Monthly*, July 1866, 1–11.

Moore, Robin. *The Green Berets.* New York: Crown, 1965.

Morris, Errol. "Liar, Liar, Pants on Fire." *New York Times*, online commentary, July 10, 2007. http://opinionator.blogs.nytimes.com/2007/07/10/pictures-are-supposed-to-be-worth-a-thousand-words/.

———. *Which Came First, the Chicken or the Egg? New York Times*, online

commentary, September 25, 2007. http://opinionator.blogs.nytimes.
com/2007/09/25/which-came-first-the-chicken-or-the-egg-part-one/.

Mullan, John. *Sentiment and Sociability: The Language of Feeling in the Eighteenth
Century.* Oxford: Clarendon Press, 1988.

O'Brien, Tim. *If I Die in a Combat Zone.* New York: Dell, 1973.

———. "How to Tell a True War Story." *The Things They Carried: A Work of Fiction.*
New York: Broadway, 1998. 67–85.

———. "The Vietnam in Me." *New York Times Magazine,* October 2, 1994,
229–38.

Owen, Wilfred. *The Complete Poems and Fragments.* Ed. J. Stallworthy. New York:
Norton, 1984.

Panzer, Mary. *Mathew Brady and the Image of History.* Washington, DC:
Smithsonian Institution Press, 1997.

Poltergeist. Dir. Tobe Hooper. Perf. JoBeth Williams, Heather O'Rourke, Craig T.
Nelson. Metro-Goldwyn-Mayer, 1982.

Prstojević, Miroslav, Željko Puljić, Maja Ražović, Aleksandra Wagner, and Bora
Ćosić. *Sarajevo Survival Guide.* Sarajevo: Work Man Publishing, 1994.

Puiseux, Hélène. *Les figures de la guerre: Représentations et sensibilités, 1839–1996.*
Paris: Gallimard, 1997.

Ramachandran, V. S., and William Hirstein. "The Perception of Phantom
Limbs. The D. O. Hebb Lecture." *Brain* 121 (1998): 1603–30.

Rancière, Jacques. *La mésentente: Politique et philosophie.* Paris: Galilée, 1995.

Rancière, Jacques. *Disagreement: Politics and Philosophy.* Trans. J. Rose.
Minneapolis: University of Minnesota Press, 2004.

Recuperati, Gianluigi. *Fucked Up.* Afterword M. Belpoliti. Milano: BUR, 2006.

Roberts, Adam. "Lives and Statistics: Are 90% of War Victims Civilians?"
Survival 52.3 (2010): 115–36.

Rousseau, Jean-Jacques. "Discourse on the Origin and Foundations of Inequality."
In *The First and Second Discourses,* 77–181. Ed. R. D. Masters. Trans. R. D.
Masters and J. R. Masters. New York: St. Martin's Press, 1964.

———. *Discours sur les sciences et les arts; Discours sur l'origine de l'inégalité.* Ed. J. Roger.
Paris: Garnier Flammarion, 1971.

Joe Sacco. *Palestine.* Intro. E. Said. Seattle: Fantagraphics, 1994.

———. *Safe Area Goražde: The War in Eastern Bosnia, 1992–1995.* Intro. C. Hitchens.
Seattle: Fantagraphics, 2000.

Sadkovich, James J. *The U.S. Media and Yugoslavia, 1991–1995*. Westport, CT: Praeger, 1998.

Sante, Luc. "Torturers and Tourists." *New York Times*, May 11, 2004.

Sarhandi, Daoud, and Alina Boboc. *Evil Doesn't Live Here: Posters from the Bosnian War*. Intro. D. Rohde. New York: Princeton Architectural Press, 2001.

Said, Edward. *Orientalism*. New York: Vintage, 1979.

Sedgwick, Eve Kosofsky. *Between Men: English Literature and Male Homosocial Desire*. New York: Columbia University Press, 1985.

Silber, Laura, and Allan Little. *Yugoslavia: Death of a Nation*. London: Penguin, 1997.

Sladoje, Igor. "United States Foreign Policy in Bosnia and Herzegovina, Somalia, Rwanda and Kosovo: Waiting and Watching." American Studies Diploma Thesis, Smith College, 2003.

Slotkin, Richard. *Regeneration through Violence: The Mythology of the American Frontier, 1600–1860*. Middletown, CT: Wesleyan University Press, 1973.

Smith, Adam. *The Theory of Moral Sentiments*. Ed. D. D. Raphael and A. L. Macfie. Oxford: Clarendon Press, 1976.

Sontag, Susan. *On Photography*. New York: Farrar, Straus & Giroux, 1977.

———. *Regarding the Pain of Others*. New York: Farrar, Straus & Giroux, 2003.

Spelman, Elizabeth V. *Fruits of Sorrow: Framing Our Attention to Suffering*. Boston: Beacon Press, 1997.

Standard Operating Procedure. Dir. Errol Morris. Perf. Megan Ambuhl Graner, Christopher Bradley, Javal Davis. Sony Pictures Classics, 2008.

Stowe, Harriet Beecher. *Uncle Tom's Cabin; or, Life among the Lowly*. Ed. E. Ammons. New York: Norton, 2010.

Sudetic, Chuck. *Blood and Vengeance: One Family's Story of the War in Bosnia*. New York: Penguin, 1998.

Tasso, Torquato. *Jerusalem Delivered (Gerusalemme liberata)*. Ed. and trans. A. M. Esolen. Baltimore: Johns Hopkins University Press, 2000.

Todorova, Maria. *Imagining the Balkans*. New York: Oxford University Press, 1997.

Traubel, Horace. *With Walt Whitman in Camden*. New York: Rowman & Littlefield, 1961.

Ugrešić, Dubravka. "Old Men and Their Grandchildren." Trans. Celia Hawkesworth. *Massachusetts Review* 52.3/4 (2011): 524–31.

Venturi, Robert, Denise Scott Brown, and Steven Izenour. *Learning from Las Vegas*. Cambridge: MIT Press, 1972.

Verbitsky, Horacio. *The Flight*. New York: New Press, 1996.

Wetzell, Richard F. Review of *Probing the Limits of Representation*, by Saul
    Friedlander. *History of European Ideas* 21.1 (1995): 87–88.

White, Hayden. "Historical Emplotment and the Problem of Truth in Historical
    Representation." *Figural Realism: Studies in the Mimesis Effect*. Baltimore:
    Johns Hopkins University Press, 1999.

Whitman, Walt. *Memoranda during the War*. Ed. P. Coviello. New York: Oxford
    University Press, 2004.

———. *Poetry and Prose*. Ed. Justin Kaplan. New York: Library of America, 1996.

WNYC. *Radio Lab*. See Abrumrad and Krulwich.

Zuckerman, Ethan. "Unpacking Kony 2012." *my heart's in acera*. www
    .ethanzuckerman.com/blog/2012/03/08/unpacking-kony-2012/.

Index

abolitionist movement, 8
Abu Ghraib, 135; interrogations, 114–
15, 140; investigation of, 115–16;
photos of, 114–16
The Abu Ghraib Effect (Eisenman), 114
activist media. See war journalism
Afghanistan War, 70, 106–7, 116
aggressors: as heroes, 109–12, 138; as
humans, 114–16; as narrators, 59,
63–64; as observers, 130–32, 150–
57; point of view, 95, 107–9, 113–14;
psychology of, 113–14, 117–23;
state-sanctioned, 115–22; violence
of, xiv, 25–26, 28–29
air strikes: in Iraq, 129–32, 148; in
Pakistan, 129; in Vietnam, 129. See
also military interventions
Albahari, David, 157–65; Götz and Meyer,
157–65
Albee, Edward, 141
Alić, Fikret, 74
al-Jamadi, Manadel, 140
al-Majid, Ali Hassan, 130–31
al-Qaeda, 129
Améry, Jean (Hanns Chaim Mayer),
139–40
amputation, 1, 5, 17–22; humor in
Bosnian War, 68; in Sontag, 45–47
Anderson, Benedict, 21
Andrić, Ivo: The Bridge on the Drina, 104
Antietam, 48

antiwar art, 114; film, 109–12. See also
war films
AP, 140
apophasis, 47
Arendt, Hannah, 16; on compassion,
7–8; The Human Condition, 7; On
Revolution, 7
Argentina: dirty war, 117–22; junta, 119
Arkan. See Ražnatović, Željko
Arnautalić, Ismet. See SaGA
artistic engagement, 44, 145–46, 149–
57; in wartime Sarajevo, xi, 42,
61–65, 145–46
Ashley-Cooper, Anthony, 30
Atlantic Monthly, 1

Balkan Ghosts (Kaplan), 34–38
Balkanism, 37–39
Balkans, 34, 37. See also individual countries
Bašić, Adisa: "Trauma Market," x–xi
Battle of the Somme, 51
Baudrillard, Jean, 69–70, 123
"Beat! Beat! Drums!" (Whitman), 12
Beyond the Pleasure Principle (Freud),
122–23
Bijeljina, 26–27, 33–34
Bilal, Wafaa: death of brother and
father, 147–49; early life, 142–44;
refugee camp life, 144–46;
relationship with brother, 147–48;
relationship with father, 143–44

—Works: *Domestic Tension*, 142, 146,
149–58; exhibition setup, 150; Digg
Day, 153–57; reactions, 152; *Shoot an
Iraqi*, 141–57, 163–65
Bill Moyers Journal, 129
body: and mind, 15, 18; mutilation of,
17–18, 63, 131–33; in pain, 1–2,
5–12, 15; understanding of, 20–21
body politic, 17, 20
Bosnia-Herzegovina, x; in Cohen,
38–40; truth commission, 158
Bosnian War, 38, 45, 59–76, 93–104,
107–9, 158; civilian victims in
Bijeljina, 25–27, 33–34; civilian
victims in Prijedor, 71–76; civilian
victims in Sarajevo, 39–41; humor,
62, 68; NATO intervention, 100–101;
Serbian paramilitary activities in,
33; Srebrenica genocide, 39. *See also*
Sarajevo
Brady, Mathew: archive of
photographs, 49; *The Dead of
Antietam*, 48–49; Washington, D.C.,
studio, 48, 82, 90
Breton, André, 6
The Bridge on the Drina (Andrić), 104

Calvino, Italo: *Memos for the Next
Millennium*, 76–79; on storytelling
method, 76–77
"The Case of George Dedlow"
(Mitchell), 1–2
Cambodia, 54
Caruth, Cathy, 122–23
Central African Republic, 128
Chancellorsville, 49
Charming Hostess: "Death is a Job,"
67; "Imam Bey's Mosque," 66;
Sarajevo Blues, 65–68
Civil War: battlefields, 12, 49, 82–87,
90; military hospitals, 1, 3–4, 14–18;
photography, 48–49, 82–92; prison
camps, 12

Clinton, Bill: and *Balkan Ghosts*, 37;
nonintervention in Bosnian War,
34–35; in Sacco, 104
CNN, 101; CNN effect, 73, 116
Coetzee, J. M.: *Diary of a Very Bad Year*,
11–12; on shame, 11; *Waiting for the
Barbarians*, 134–41, 151, 163–64
Cohen, Roger: *Hearts Grown Brutal: Sagas
of Sarajevo*, 38–41, 55–58
Colbert, Stephen, 70–71, 75
Cole, Teju, 125, 127–28
collateral damage, 9, 15
compassion: Arendt on, 7–8; Mandeville
on, 31; in Mehmedinović, 60; nature
of, 7, 25–30; Rousseau on, 31;
Spelman on, 8–9
competitiveness, 27
Confederacy. *See* Civil War.
Congo, Democratic Republic of the,
128
"Corpse" (Mehmedinović), 60–61
Cortázar, Julio, 119–20
critics, literary. *See* literary criticism
Croatian War, 102, 157

Damasio, Antonio, 15
Dani, 58
The Dead of Antietam (Brady), 48–49
Dead Troops Talk (Wall), 45
"Death is a Job" (Charming Hostess),
67
Debord, Guy, 69–70
Deichmann, Thomas, 79, 81, 92; "The
Photo That Fooled the World,"
73–76
"The Devil and the Rose"
(Mehmedinović), 58–61
Diary of a Very Bad Year (Coetzee), 11–12
Digg.com, 153–57
Disasters of War (Goya), 18
Discourse on Inequality (Rousseau), 25
Dispatches (Herr), 7, 44–45, 109, 113–14
Domestic Tension (Bilal), 142, 146, 149–57

Doody, Margaret, 36
Drew, Elizabeth, 34
Drljača, Simo, 71–73
drone warfare, 129–32; description of, 131
"Drum-Taps" (Whitman), 1

Eisenberg, Jewlia. See Charming Hostess
Eisenman, Stephen: The Abu Ghraib Effect, 114
Elliott, Jane, 159–60
emancipation, 8
ethnic cleansing, in Bijeljina, 26–27, 33–34

The Fable of Bees (Mandeville), 26
FAMA: Sarajevo Survival Guide, 61–62, 145–46; Sarajevo Survival Map, 61
Fenton, Roger, 82–87
First World War. See World War I
Flaying of Marsyas (Titian), 9–10
former Yugoslavia. See Yugoslavia, former
Frassanito, William, 82–87
Fredericksburg, 1
Fresh Air, 130–32
Freud, Sigmund, 41, 64; Beyond the Pleasure Principle, 122–23
Friedlander, Saul, 92–93
Frontline, 159–60
Fussell, Paul: The Great War and Modern Memory, 50–51, 106

Gardner, Alexander, 82–85, 89–92; "Harvest of Death," 82, 90; Photographic Sketch Book of the War, 82; "Sharpshooter's Home," 91–92; "A Sharpshooter's Last Sleep" 90–92
Garlasco, Marc, 130–32
genocide: in Bosnia-Herzegovina, 39; in Cambodia, 54; in Rwanda, xiii, 21, 54

Gestapo, 139–40
Gettysburg, 82–85
Ginzburg, Carlo, 125, 164
Glover, Jonathan, 9–10, 157; Humanity, 136, 146
Gonzales, Alberto, 116
Goražde, 95–104
Gorman, Erna, 117–18
gothic fiction, 36–37
Götz and Meyer (Albahari), 157–65
Gourevitch, Philip: on Rwanda, 21; Standard Operating Procedure, 116
Goya, Francisco: Disasters of War, 18
graphic novels. See war graphic novels
The Great War and Modern Memory (Fussell), 50–51, 106
greed, 27
Greek myths, 77–79, 89
The Green Berets (Wayne), 109–12
Greene, Joshua, 87–89, 128
Gross, Terry, 130
Guantanamo prison, 116
Guardian, 71
Gulf of Tonkin incident, 129
Gulf War, 141–46, 148; refugee camps, 144–46

Hadžihalilović, Bojan. See TRIO
Hadžihalilović, Dada. See TRIO
Hague, the. See ICTY
Hampshire College, 107
Hanley, Lynne, 54
Hardoin, Eric, 39
"Harvest of Death" (Gardner), 82, 90
Haviv, Ron, 26, 32–34, 73
Hearts Grown Brutal: Sagas of Sarajevo (Cohen), 38–41, 55–58
Herak, Borislav, 62–64
heroes, 26, 40–41, 157; and aggressors, 108; aggressors becoming, 138; becoming victims, 138–40
Herr, Michael, 44–48; Dispatches, 7, 44–45, 109, 113–14

history: and language, xiii; and myth,
    76; and violence, 105
Hobbes, Thomas, 27, 36
Holmes, Oliver Wendell, Sr., 48
Holocaust, 92–93, 117–18, 158–63
"How to Tell a True War Story"
    (O'Brien), 80–81, 112–13
The Human Condition (Arendt), 7
human rights organizations, 23, 126.
    See also entries for individual
    organizations
Human Rights Watch, 116, 127–28, 163
Humanity (Glover), 136, 146
Hume, David: on compassion, 29–30;
    Treatise of Human Nature, 29
humor: Bosnian war, 62, 68; satire, xi
Hussein, Saddam, 130, 143
Hutu Power Radio, xiii

ICTY, 71–73, 158
Idrizović, Mirza. *See* SaGA
If I Die in a Combat Zone (O'Brien), 43
Ignatieff, Michael: *Virtual War*, 32, 69
Illich, Ivan, 11
"Imam Bey's Mosque" (Charming
    Hostess), 66
"Imam of the Bey Mosque"
    (Mehmedinović), 65–66
Incidents in the Life of a Slave Girl (Jacobs),
    8–9
injury: physical, 1–2, 5, 9, 15, 39–41;
    psychological, 20. *See also* pain;
    suffering
International Criminal Tribunal for the
    Former Yugoslavia. *See* ICTY
International Red Cross, 74
international response to Bosnian War,
    xi, 31–32
interpreters, 95–99
Invisible Children, 126–28, 158
Iraq, 141–49; Gulf War, 141–47, 148;
    Gulf War refugee camps, 144–47;
    Iraq War, 11, 70, 106–7, 114–16,

130–33, 147–49; Iraq War in film,
    20; Iraq War in media, 101
irony, 28; and nihilism, 47; and
    sentimentality, 30; and war, 50–51
ITN, 71, 73–75

Jacobs, Harriet, 15–16; *Incidents in the
    Life of a Slave Girl*, 8–9
Jajinci mass burial site, 158–62
Jergović□, Miljenko, 68
Jerusalem Delivered (Tasso), 122–23
Johnson, Lyndon B., 129–30

Kant, Immanuel, 9; on torture, 10
Kaplan, Robert, 34–35, 37; *Balkan
    Ghosts*, 34–38; narrative method,
    35–36
Kebo, Ozren, x
Keesey, Ben. *See* Invisible Children
Kenović, Ademir. *See* SaGA
Keraterm prison camp, 71–72
King, Martin Luther, Jr., assassination
    of, 159–60
Kony, Joseph, 126–29, 163
Kony 2012 video, 125–29, 158, 163;
    reactions to, 127–28; second video,
    128
Kosovar Albanians, 23
Kosovo, 23, 32
Kosovo War, 23, 69; civilian casualties,
    32; "Madonna of the Refugees"
    image, 23–25, 31; military
    participants, 32; refugee crisis,
    23–24
Kristof, Nicholas D., 127–28, 163
Krulwich, Robert, 88

Lacoue-Labarthe, Philippe, 36; "Nazi
    Myth," 23
Larkin, Philip: *MCMXIV*, 106
Latour, Bruno: "Why Has Critique Run
    Out of Steam?," 69, 75
Leaves of Grass (Whitman), 3–4, 12, 15

Lebowitz, Fran, xi–xii
L'Enfant, Pierre, 4
Lehrer, Jonah, 15
Les figures de la guerre (Puiseux), 69–70
Levey, Gregory, 11
Levi, Primo, 93
Library of Congress, 85
Limbaugh, Rush, 114–15
Lincoln, Abraham, 4, 8, 90, 92
literary criticism, importance of, xii, 75
literature of sensibility. See
    sentimentalism
Living Marxism, 73–76
Lord's Resistance Army. See Kony,
    Joseph
Love Thy Neighbor (Maass), 107–9
Lydersen, Kari, 141–42; Shoot an Iraqi,
    141–57, 163–65

Maass, Peter, 112, 121; Love Thy Neighbor,
    107–9
Mahdi Army, 148
Mandeville, Bernard de, 30–32, 34, 37,
    126; on compassion, 31; The Fable of
    Bees, 26
Marker, Chris, 69
McGuirk, Carol, 26
MCMXIV (Larkin), 106
Meadlo, Paul, 80
media coverage: Bosnian War, xi,
    69–70, 101; Southern Cone wars, xi;
    Vietnam War, xi, 80. See also war
    journalism
Mehmedinović, Semezdin: on
    Charming Hostess, 68; "Corpse,"
    60–61; "The Devil and the Rose,"
    58–61; "Imam of the Bey Mosque,"
    65–66; Sarajevo Blues, 57–58, 60, 65;
    "Shelter," 66–67
Memoranda during the War (Whitman), 16
Memos for the Next Millennium (Calvino),
    76–79
Menem, Carlos, 118–19

MGM Sarajevo (SaGA), 62–65;
    soundtrack, 64
military aid, in Uganda, 127
military interventions: in Bosnia-
    Herzegovina, 34–35, 39, 95–99; in
    Kosovo, 23–25, 31–32, 157
Miller, Geoffrey, Major General, 116
mind and body, 15
minstrel shows, 154
Mitchell, S. Weir, 18; "The Case of
    George Dedlow," 1–2
Mladi□, Ratko, 63
modernism, 93
moral behavior, research on, 87
Morris, Errol, 81–82, 116
Morrison, Norman, 11
Moyers, Bill, 129
Mulabegovi□, Lejla. See TRIO
Mullan, John, 29
Muqtada al-Sadr, 148
My Lai Massacre, 79–80, 112

Nancy, Jean-Luc, 36; "Nazi Myth," 23
nation, existence of, 21
National Public Radio. See NPR
nationalism, 21, 38
NATO, 32, 39. See also military
    interventions
"Nazi Myth" (Lacoue-Labarthe and
    Nancy), 23
neorealism, 76, 78
neuroscience, 18–21; moral dilemmas,
    87–89, 146; phenomena, 1
New York Times, 26, 32, 38, 81, 127, 129;
    style of war reporting, 54–55
New Yorker, 140
Newsday, 71
nowthatsfuckedup.com, 132–33
NPR, xi, 88, 130–32

"O Captain! My Captain!" (Whitman),
    12
object, 47. See also victims

O'Brien, Tim, 44–48, 50; "How to Tell a True War Story," 80–81, 112–13; *If I Die in a Combat Zone*, 43; *The Things They Carried*, 80

observers, 17, 93–104; and aggressors, 58–59, 107–9, 150–57, 161; American citizens as, 70–71; compassionate, 31, 92, 107, 115; disgust of, 113–14; helplessness of, xiv, 25–28; and victims, 29–30, 40–41, 161–62

Omarska prison camp, 71–72

On Revolution (Arendt), 7

Operation Desert Storm. *See* Iraq: Gulf War

Orientalism (Said), 38

Orwell, George, 136–37, 151

O'Sullivan, Timothy, 82–87

Owen, Wilfred: "Dulce et Decorum Est," 51–53; writing style, 51

Page, Tim, 109

pain: as instrument, 135, 139, 155–56; phantom limb, 1–2, 19–21. *See also* injury; suffering

Palestine (Sacco), 93

Panzer, Mary, 48

Patent Office, 4–7, 11, 13, 22; as *Wunderkammer*, 13–16, 21

patriotism, 20

PBS, 159–60

Pernías, Antonio, 118–19

Perseus, myth of, 77–79, 95–99, 165

phantom limbs, 21; in fiction, 1–2; in Ramachandran's experiment, 18–20

"The Photo That Fooled The World" (Deichmann), 73–76

Photographic Sketch Book of the War (Gardner), 82

Pikulić, Mladen, 57

pity. *See* compassion

postmodernism, 69–70, 76, 78, 89

Powell, Colin, 116

Predator drones. *See* drone warfare

Prijedor, 71–76

prison camps: in Bosnian War, 71–76; in Civil War, 12; in World War II, 158–60

prisoners: in Argentinian dirty war, 117–22; in Iraq War, 114–16. *See also* prison camps

prisoners' dilemma, 146

propaganda, 75, 106

psychoanalysis, 41, 45, 64, 122–23

Puiseux, Hélène: *Les figures de la guerre*, 69–70

RadioLab, 88

Ramachandran, V. S., phantom limb experiment, 18–20

Rancière, Jacques, 163–64

Ražnatović, Željko, 33

realism: in film, 69–70; in graphic novels, 93–101

refugees: of Bosnian War, 104, 158; of Civil War, 23–26; of Gulf War, 144–47; of Kosovo War, 23–24, 31

Regarding the Pain of Others (Sontag), 6–7, 17–18, 45–47, 59, 70–71, 82

rescuers. *See* heroes

Rice, Condoleezza, 116

Richardson, Samuel, 25

Ricuperati, Gianluigi, 132–33

"Rise O Days from Your Fathomless Depths" (Whitman), 12

Ritscher, Malachi, 11

Robespierre, Maximilien, 7–8

Rodrigues, Almiro, Judge, 73

Rolón, Juan Carlos, 118

Rose, Peter I., 23

Rousseau, Jean-Jacques, 25–27, 30–34, 92, 107, 126–28, 157; on compassion, 31; *Discourse on Inequality*, 25

Rumsfeld, Donald, 116

Russell, Jason, 125–28, 158; public breakdown, 128

Rwanda, xiii, 21, 54

Šabanović, Faruk, 39–41, 55–56
Sacco, Joe: *Palestine*, 93; *Safe Area Goražde*, 93–104
Safe Area Goražde (Sacco), 93–104
SaGA: *MGM Sarajevo*, 62–65
Said, Edward: *Orientalism*, 38
Sajmište concentration camp, 158–60
Sarajevo, siege of, x, 54–68, 70, 101; artistic resistance, xi, 42, 54, 61–65, 145–46; Jewish refugees, 158; Markale massacre, 39, 63–64; sniper fire, 39–41, 54–57, 66–67; shelling, 41, 54, 65–66; victim accounts, 39–41, 55–57
Sarajevo Blues (Charming Hostess), 65–68
Sarajevo Blues (Mehmedinović), 57–58, 60, 65
Sarajevo Survival Guide (FAMA), 61–62, 145
Sarajevo Survival Map (FAMA), 61
Sartre, Jean-Paul, 47
Saudi Arabia, 144–46
"The Scholars' Initiative" project, 71
Scilingo, Adolpho Francisco, 117–22
Second World War. *See* World War II
segregation, 159–60
self-immolation, 11
sentimentalism: challenging, 133–34; in contemporary war journalism, 35, 39–41; in gothic fiction, 36; power of, 126–28; result of, 42; in war stories, 25–28, 30, 32, 43, 61
September 11, 2001, xi–xii, 106
Serbia: civilian casualties, 32; military in Kosovo War, 32; paramilitary activities in Bosnia-Herzegovina, 33
Serbian Krajina, Republic of, 106
shame: for crimes, 12; and shock, 6–7, 9; as result of torture, 10–11
"Sharpshooter's Home" (Gardner), 91–92
"A Sharpshooter's Last Sleep" (Gardner), 90–92

sharpshooters. *See* snipers
"Shelter" (Mehmedinović), 66–67
Shoot an Iraqi (Bilal and Lydersen), 141–57, 163–65
Singer, P. W., 131–32
Slotkin, Richard, 12
Smith, Adam, 27–29, 34; *Theory of Moral Sentiments*, 28; *The Wealth of Nations*, 28
Smith College, 107
snipers: in Bosnian War, 39–41, 54–57, 66–67; in Civil War, 90–92
"Song of Myself" (Whitman), 3
Sontag, Susan, 12, 30, 62–64, 104; *Regarding the Pain of Others*, 6–7, 17–18, 45–47, 59, 70–71, 82; on Titian, 9
Spanish Civil War, 136–37
spectators. *See* observers
Spelman, Elizabeth: on compassion, 8–9
Sprey, Pierre, 129
Srebrenica genocide, 39
Standard Operating Procedure (Gourevitch), 116
Stein, Gertrude, 106
Sterne, Laurence, 25–26
Stowe, Harriet Beecher: *Uncle Tom's Cabin*, 8
Sudetic, Charles, 54–55
suffering: depiction of, 17–18, 36, 39–40, 48, 63–64, 90, 120–22; depiction of in art, 114–15, 152–54; spectacle of, 42, 131–33. *See also* injury; pain
surrealism, 6
sympathy. *See* compassion

Tasso, Torquato: *Jerusalem Delivered*, 122–23
Taylor, J. P., 102
Theory of Moral Sentiments (Smith), 28
The Things They Carried (O'Brien), 80

Time, 24–26, 30–32, 72–73; effect on
military interventions, 31–32
Titian (Tiziano Vecellio): *Flaying of
Marsyas*, 9–10
Tomb of the Unknown Soldier, 49–50
torture, 9–12, 107–9, 123–24; depicted
in Améry, 139–40; depicted in
Coetzee, 134–37; methods, 135,
138–40, 155–56; and pleasure, 28;
state-sanctioned, 115–24
tragedy, 25
trauma, 122–24; Freudian narrative of,
123; and injury, 20
"Trauma Market" (Bašić), x–xi
travel writing, 34–37
Treatise of Human Nature (Hume), 29
TRIO, 42
Trnopolje prison camp, 71–75
Tulić, Nermin, 41, 55

Uganda, 126–28
Uncle Tom's Cabin (Stowe), 8
UN peacekeepers, 39–41, 95
University of California, Los Angeles,
92–93
University of Massachusetts Amherst,
ix, 11
Union. *See* Civil War

Verbitsky, Horacio, 113–18
victims: aggressors becoming, 140–41;
anger of, 56–57; becoming
aggressors, 129; civilian, 26–27,
33–34, 39–41, 53–54, 71–76, 101,
131–33; giving voice to, 44, 47–48;
innocence of, xiv; and observers,
29–30, 40–41, 65; as "pathetic
object," 26, 29, 44; victim-
aggressor-observer structure, 30,
33, 54, 58–59, 133–34
Vietnam War, 25, 34, 44–45, 79–81,
106, 112–13, 129–30; in film, 109–12
violence: in history, 105; in Sontag,

45–47; as spectacle, 25–26, 42;
racist, xiii, 21, 54, 159–61. *See also*
aggressors; injury
Virtual War (Ignatieff), 32, 69
voyeurism, 6–7, 28
Vukovar, 57

Waiting for the Barbarians (Coetzee), 134–
41, 151, 163–64
Wall, Jeff: *Dead Troops Talk*, 45;
description by Sontag, 45–47
Walsh, Rodolfo, 119
war: civilian vs. military casualties,
53–54; glamour of, 109; imagery of,
6–7, 16–17, 48, 63–64; interpretation of, 44, 47–48; media coverage
of, 25. *See also entries for individual
wars*
war crimes: Argentina, 117–22; Bosnia-
Herzegovina (*see* war crimes in
Bosnia-Herzegovina); Cambodia,
54; Central African Republic, 128;
Congo, Democratic Republic of the,
128; Iraq, 114–16, 140; Rwanda, xiii,
21, 54; Uganda, 125–28; Vietnam,
79–80, 112–14
war crimes in Bosnia-Herzegovina:
Bijeljina, 26–27, 33–34; Prijedor,
71–76; Sarajevo, 39–41, 62–64;
Srebrenica, 39
war films, 69, 109–12
war graphic novels, 93–104
war journalism: in Argentinian dirty
war, 117–22; in Bosnian War, 38–41,
54–57, 69–76, 107–9; depiction of
in film, 110–11; power of, 25–26;
sentimentalism in, 35, 39–41; trust
in, 75; in Vietnam War, 79–81, 109
war photography, 9, 23, 30–31, 45–50;
Abu Ghraib (Iraq War), 114–16;
amateur, during Iraq War132–33;
Bosnian War, 26, 32–34, 57–60,
71–76; Civil War, 48–49, 82–87,

89–92; Crimean War, 82; Kosovo War, 24; manipulations, 82–92; of refugees, 23–25, 31; of Vukovar, 57
war porn, 7, 114–15, 132–33
war stories: basic structure of, xiii–xiv, 30; concerns regarding, 43–44; effectiveness of, 45; fascination with, 7, 109; importance of, 2, 17, 22; limitations of, 129–30; powers of, 79
Washington, D.C., public buildings in, 4–5, 14
Washington Post, 34, 142
Wayne, John, 109–12
The Wealth of Nations (Smith), 28
Wetzell, Richard, 92–93
"When Lilacs Last in the Dooryard Bloom'd" (Whitman), 12
White, Hayden, 92–93
Whitman, Walt: and body, 15; brother of, 2; Civil War writings, xiv, 2–4, 12, 49–50, 69; on compassion, 16; influence on Mitchell, 18; motivation in writing, 7; as national poet, 3, 92; nursing, 3, 17, 20; on Patent Office, 4–6, 13; on poetry, 2
—Works: "Beat! Beat! Drums!," 12; "Drum-Taps," 1; Leaves of Grass, 3–4,

12, 15; Memoranda during the War, 16; "O Captain! My Captain!," 12; "Rise O Days from Your Fathomless Depths," 12; "Song of Myself," 3; Specimen Days, 50; "When Lilacs Last in the Dooryard Bloom'd," 12; "The Wound-Dresser" 17–21, 161
"The Wound-Dresser" (Whitman), 17–21, 161
"Why Has Critique Run Out of Steam?" (Latour), 69, 75
Wikipedia, 71
Wilson, Chris, 123–33
witnesses. See observers
World War I, 106; poetry of, 51–54
World War II, 76, 104–6, 158–63

Young, Marilyn, 129–30
Yugoslavia, former, x, 54, 105; in Albahari, 158–65; in Cohen, 38–41; in Kaplan, 34–38. See also individual countries of former Yugoslavia
Yugoslav wars, 35, 106; consensus history of, 71. See also individual wars in former Yugoslavia

Žalica, Pjer. See SaGA
Zuckerman, Ethan, 127